THANKSGIVING

Coloring Book For Toddlers

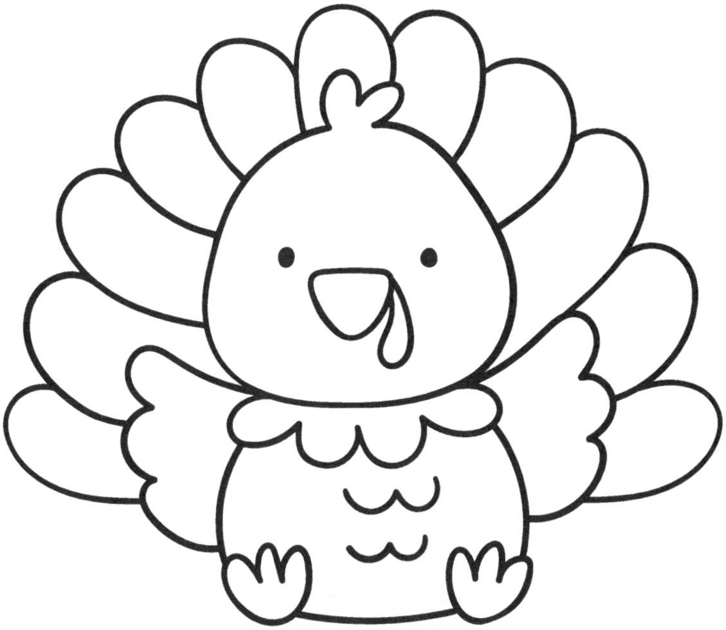

This Book Belongs To:

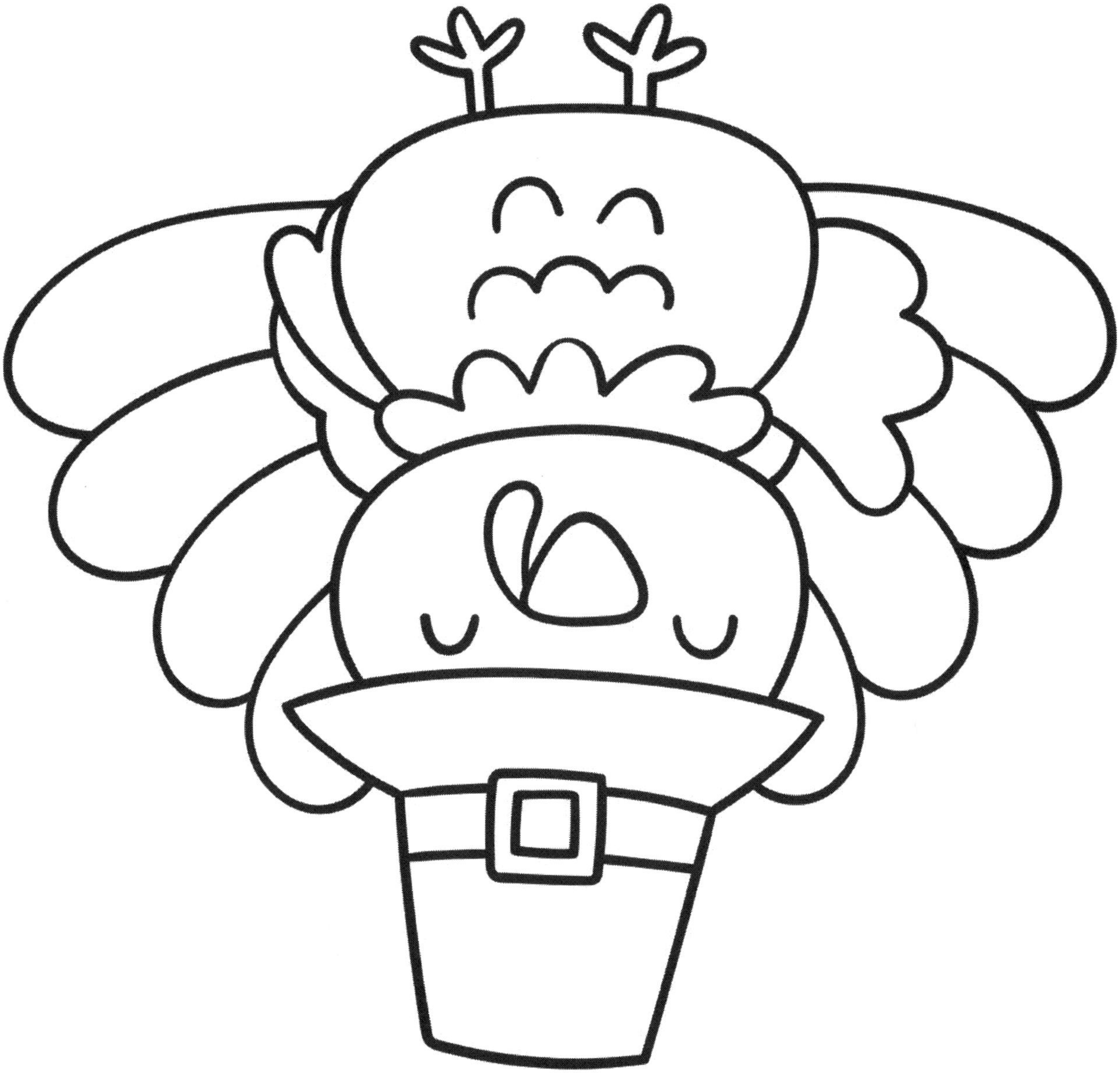

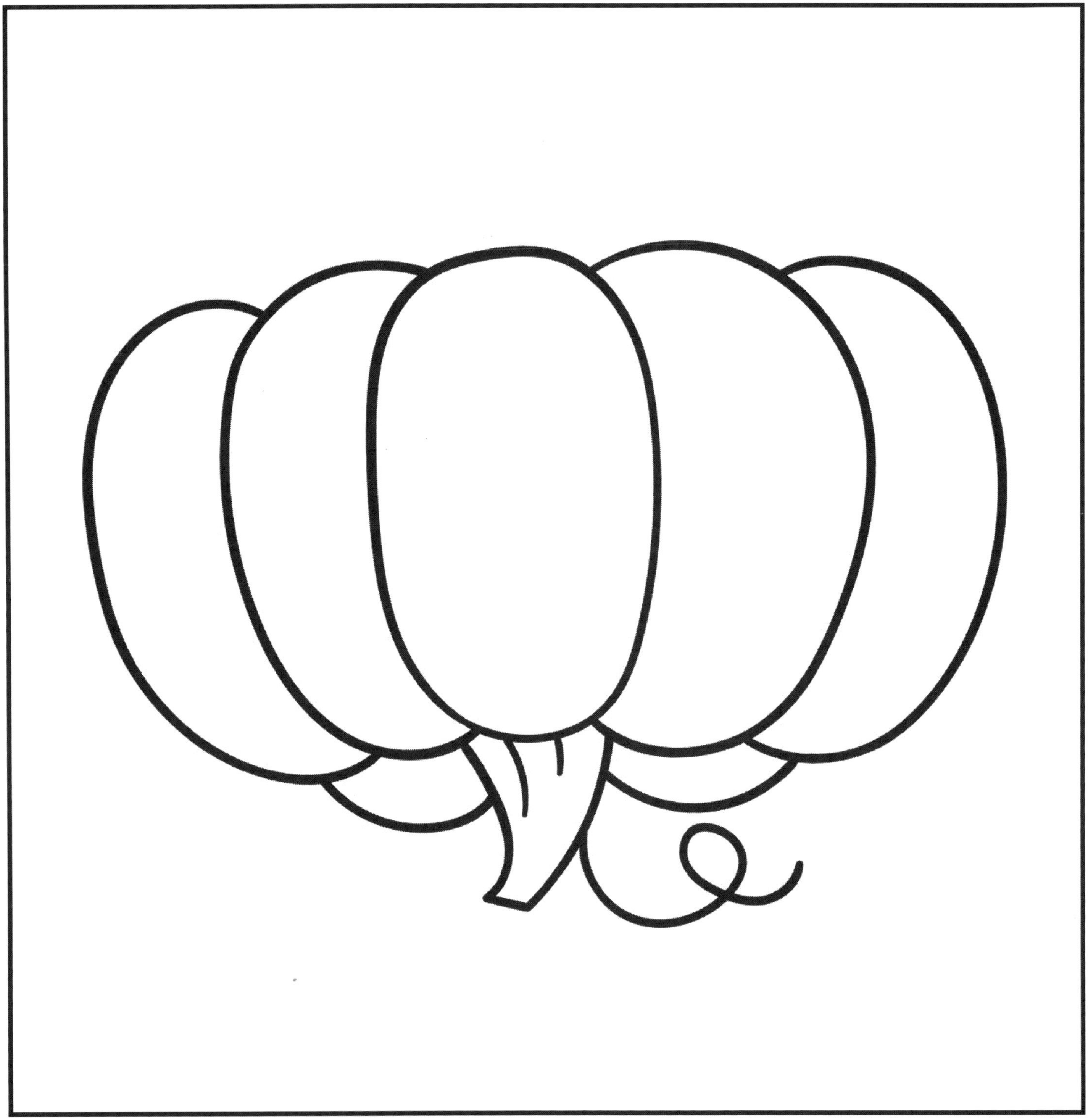

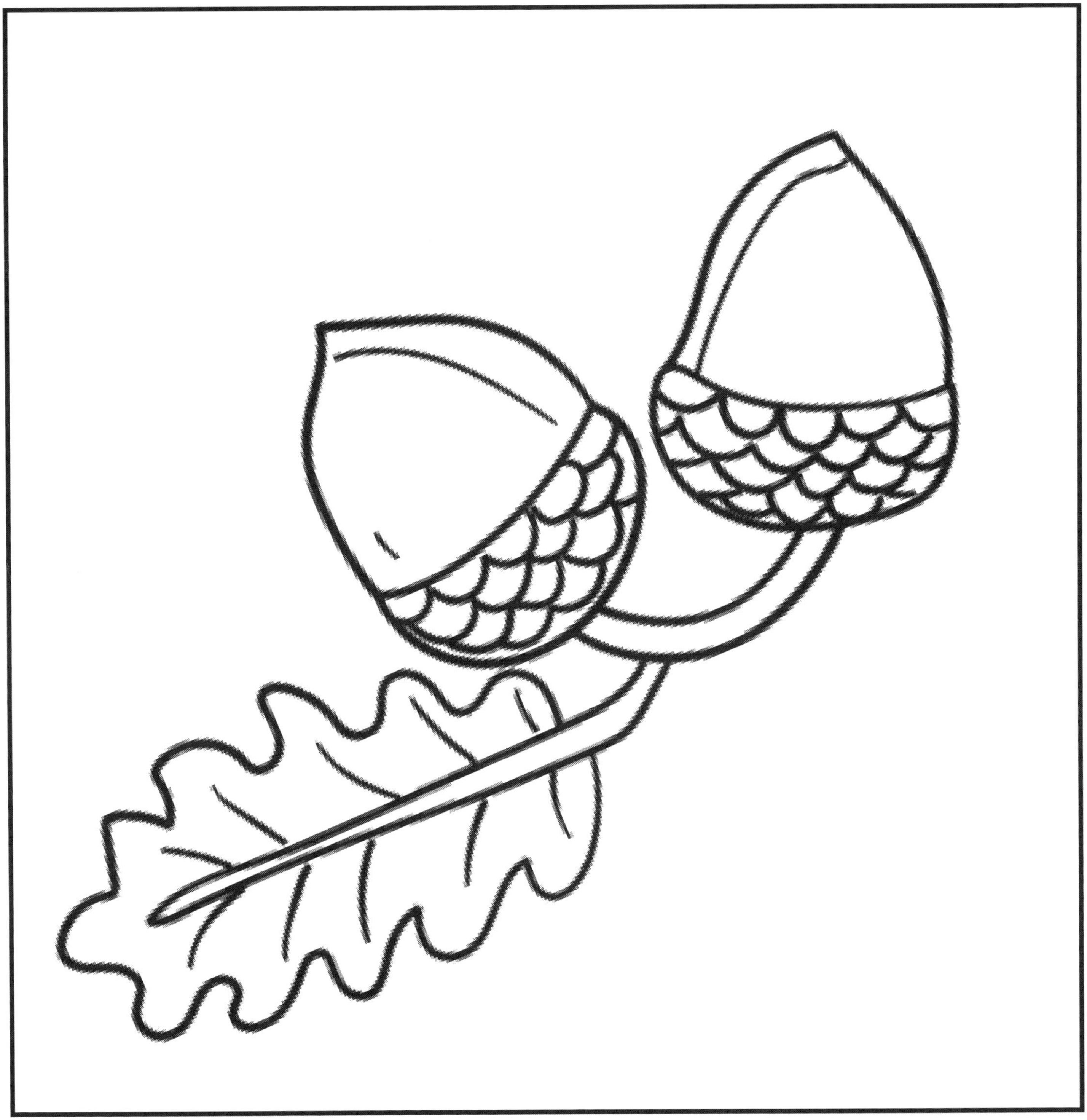

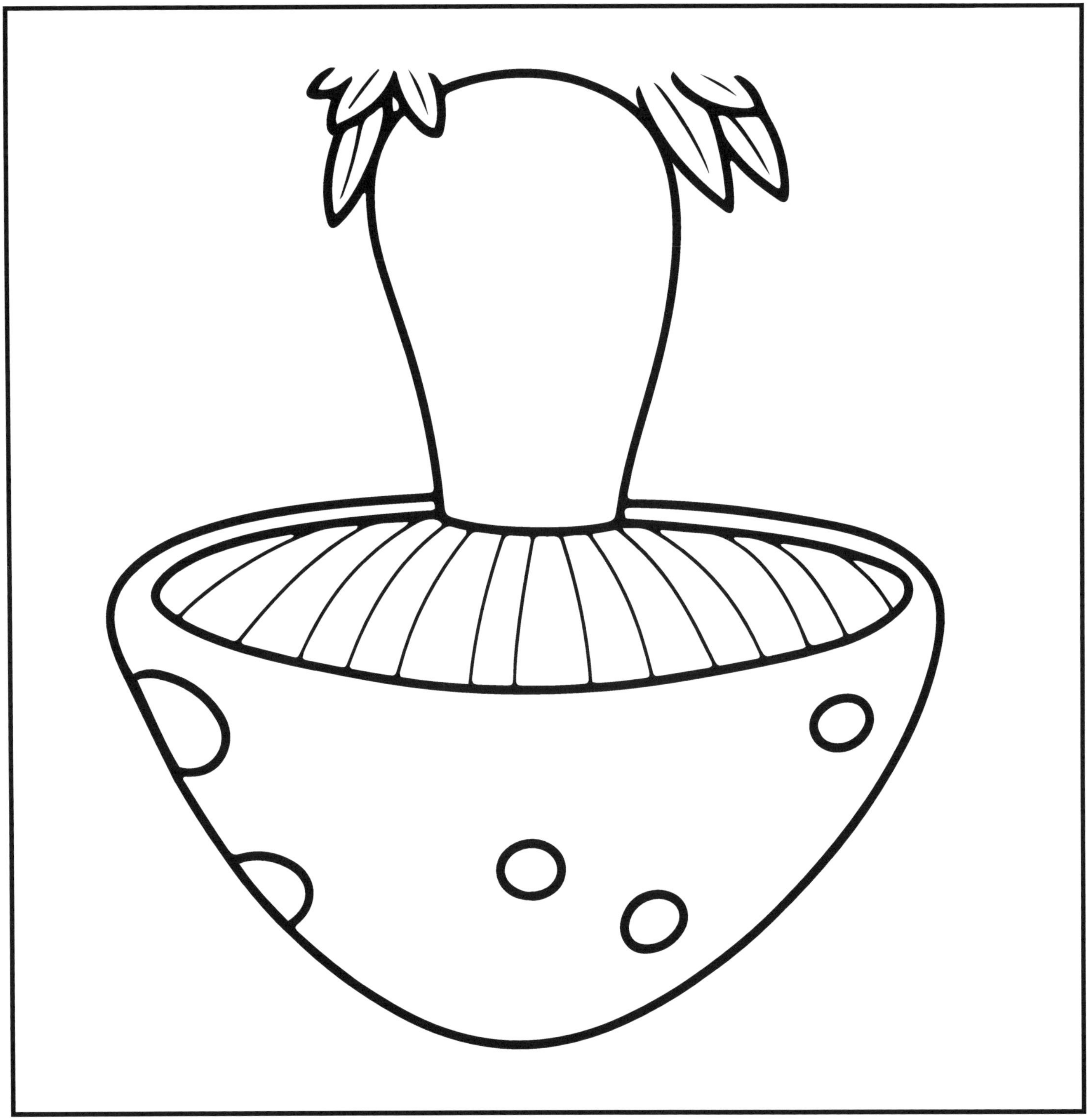

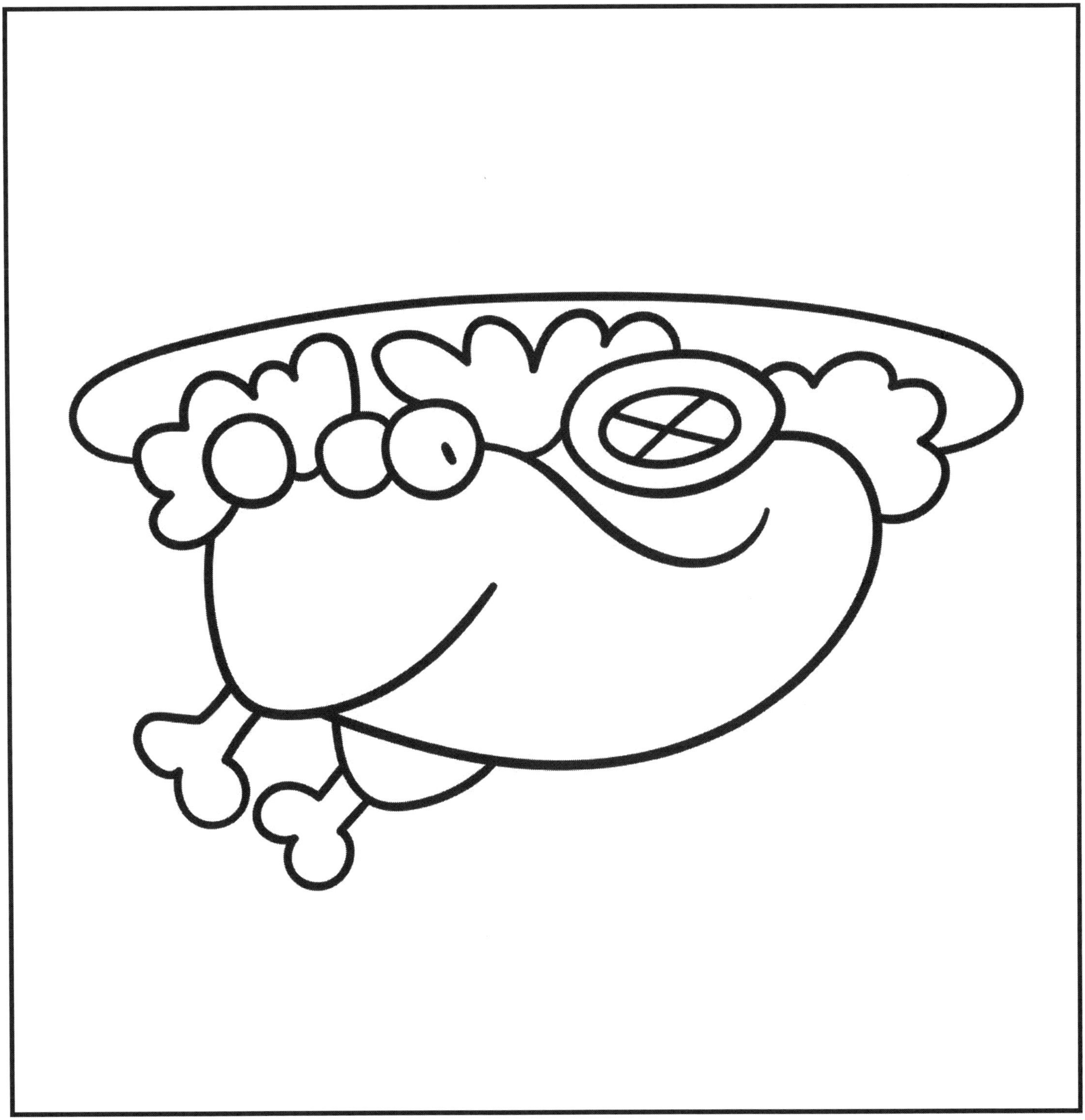

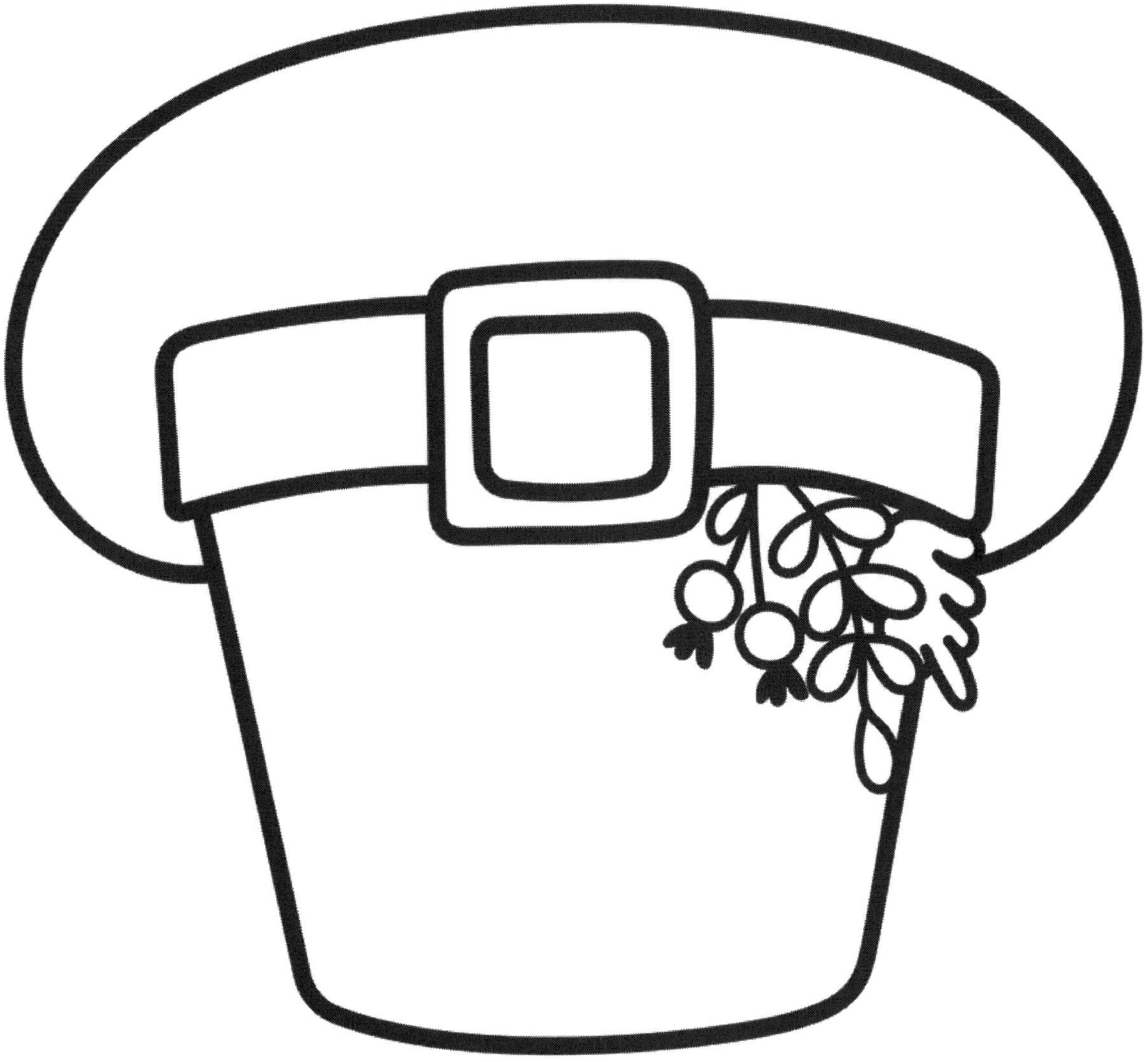

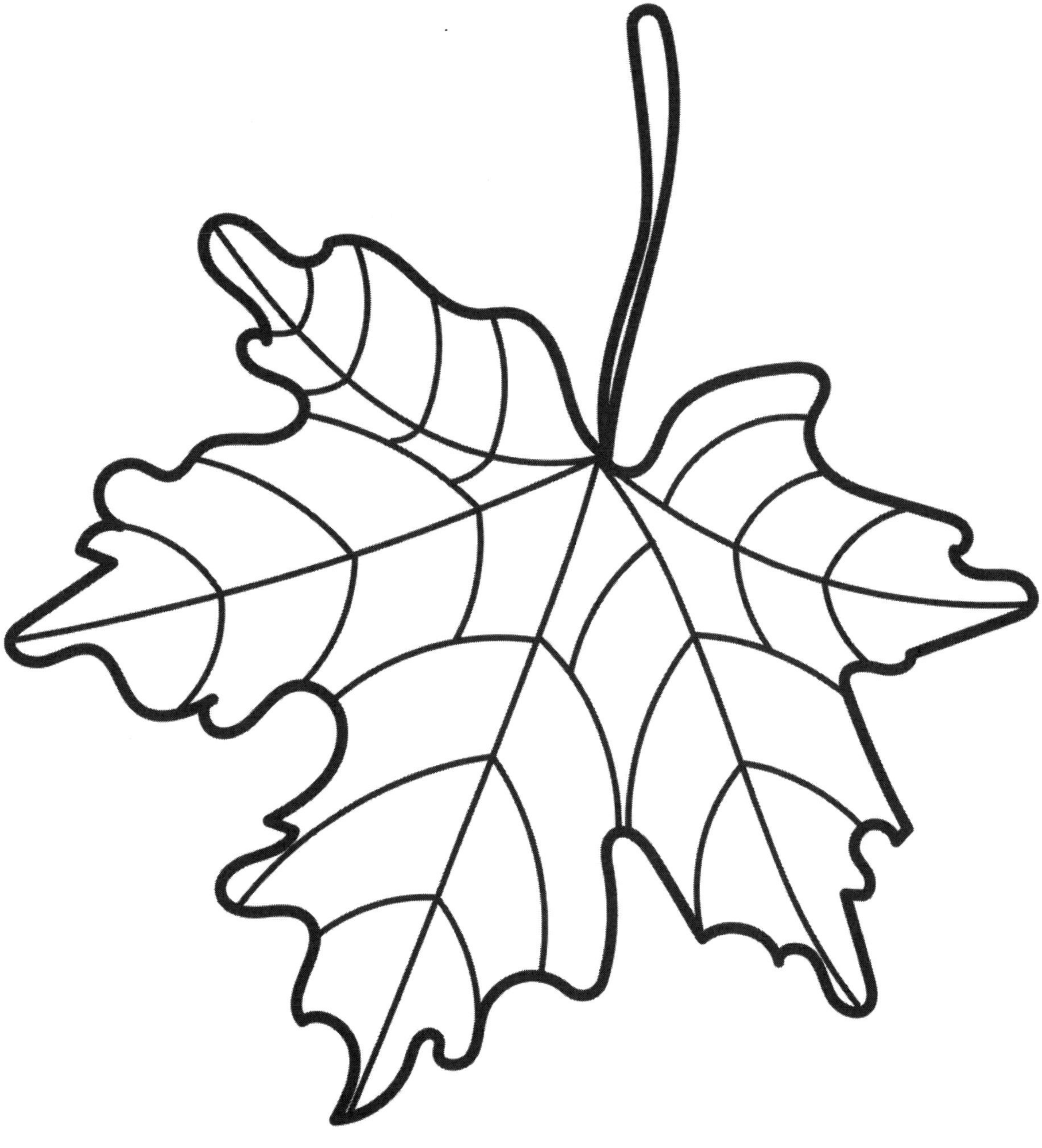

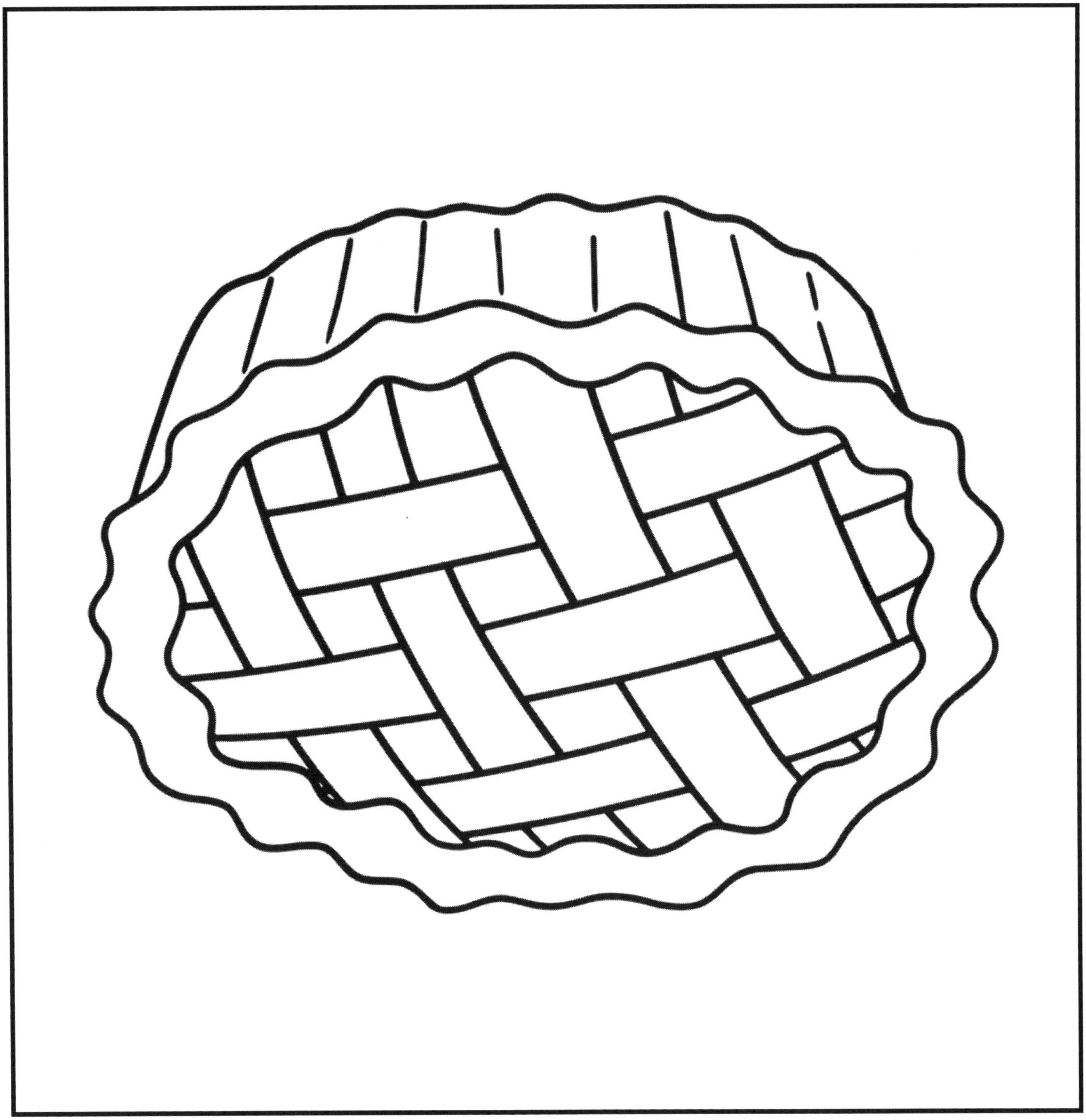

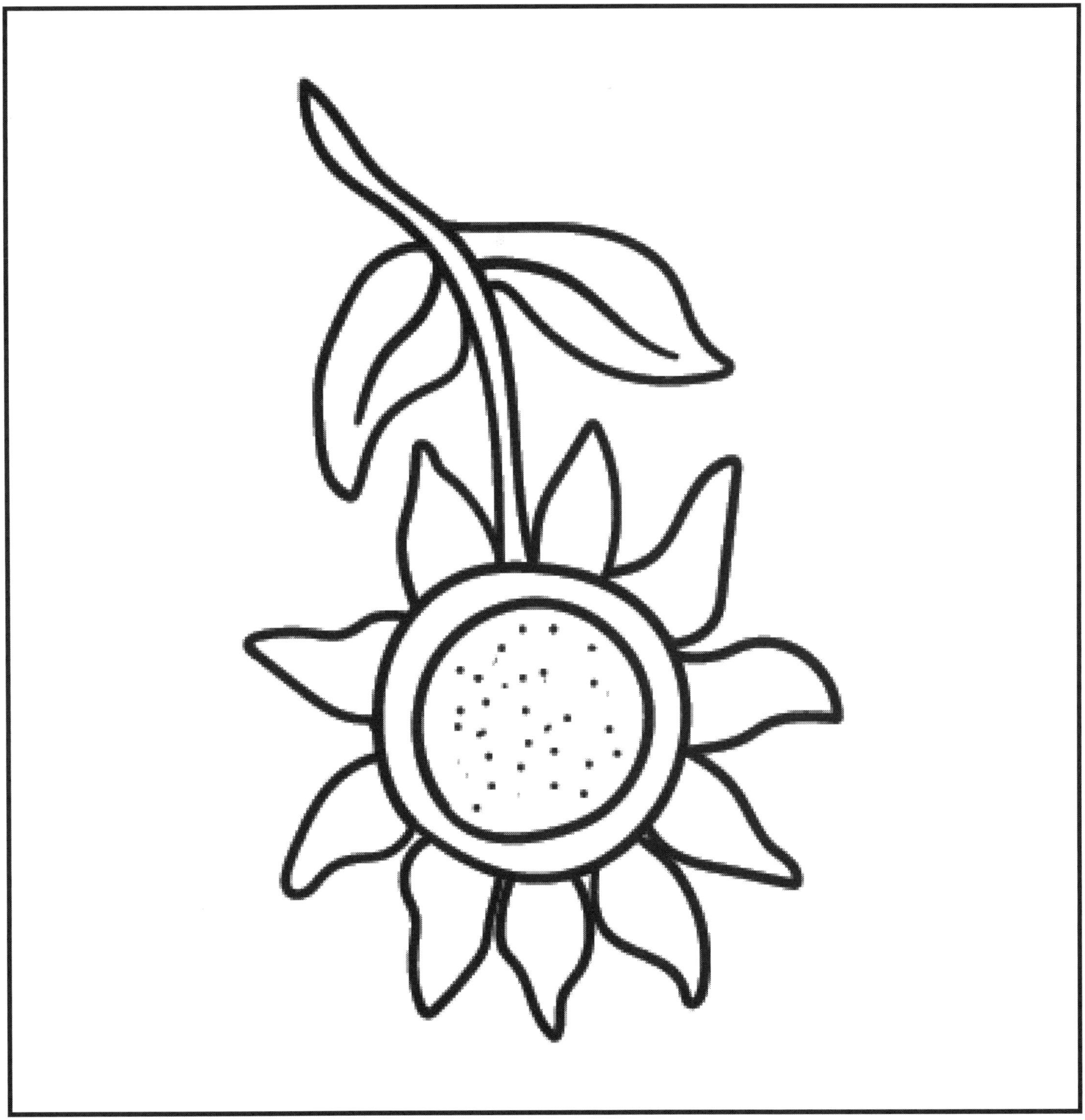

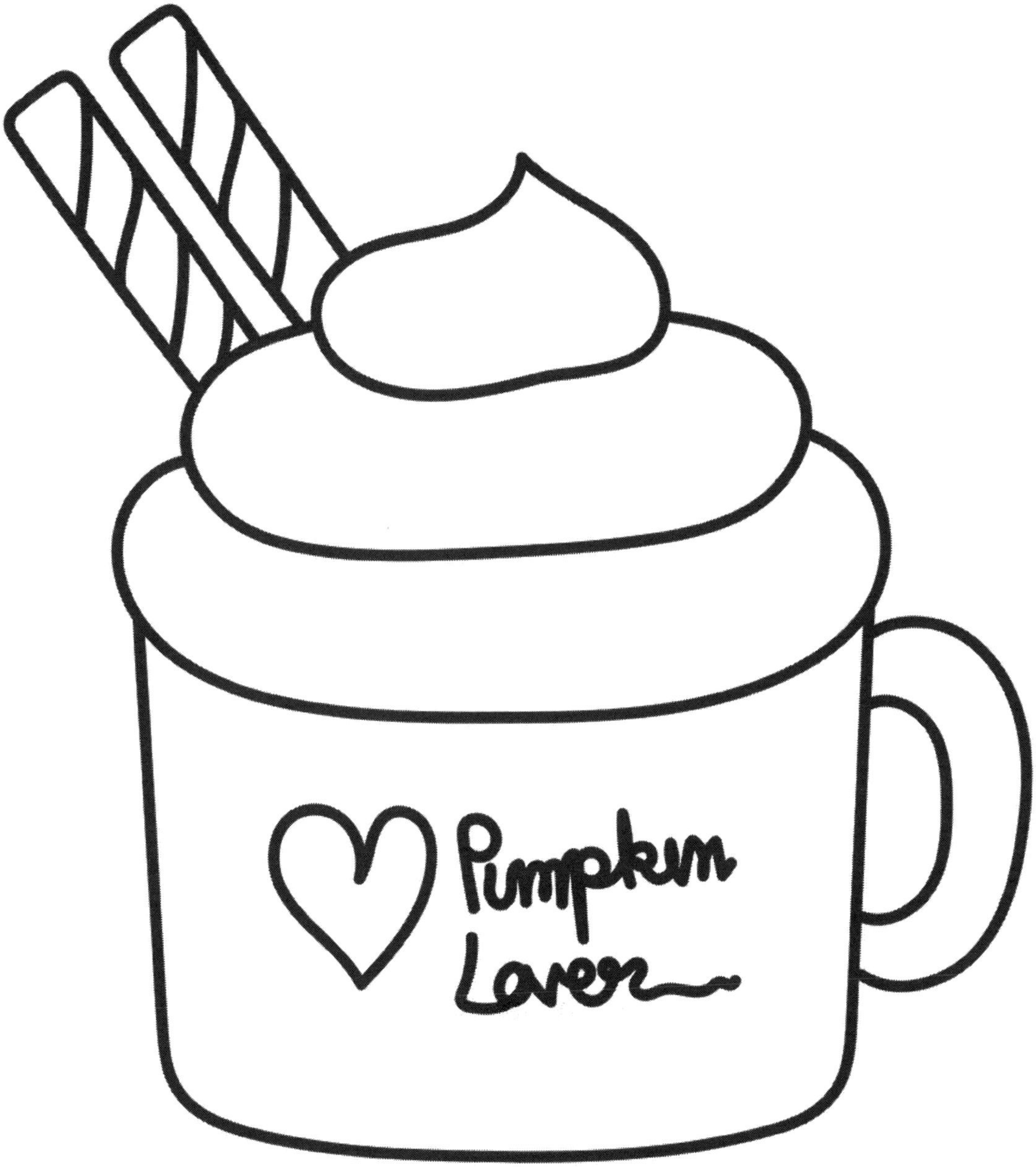
Pumpkin
Lover

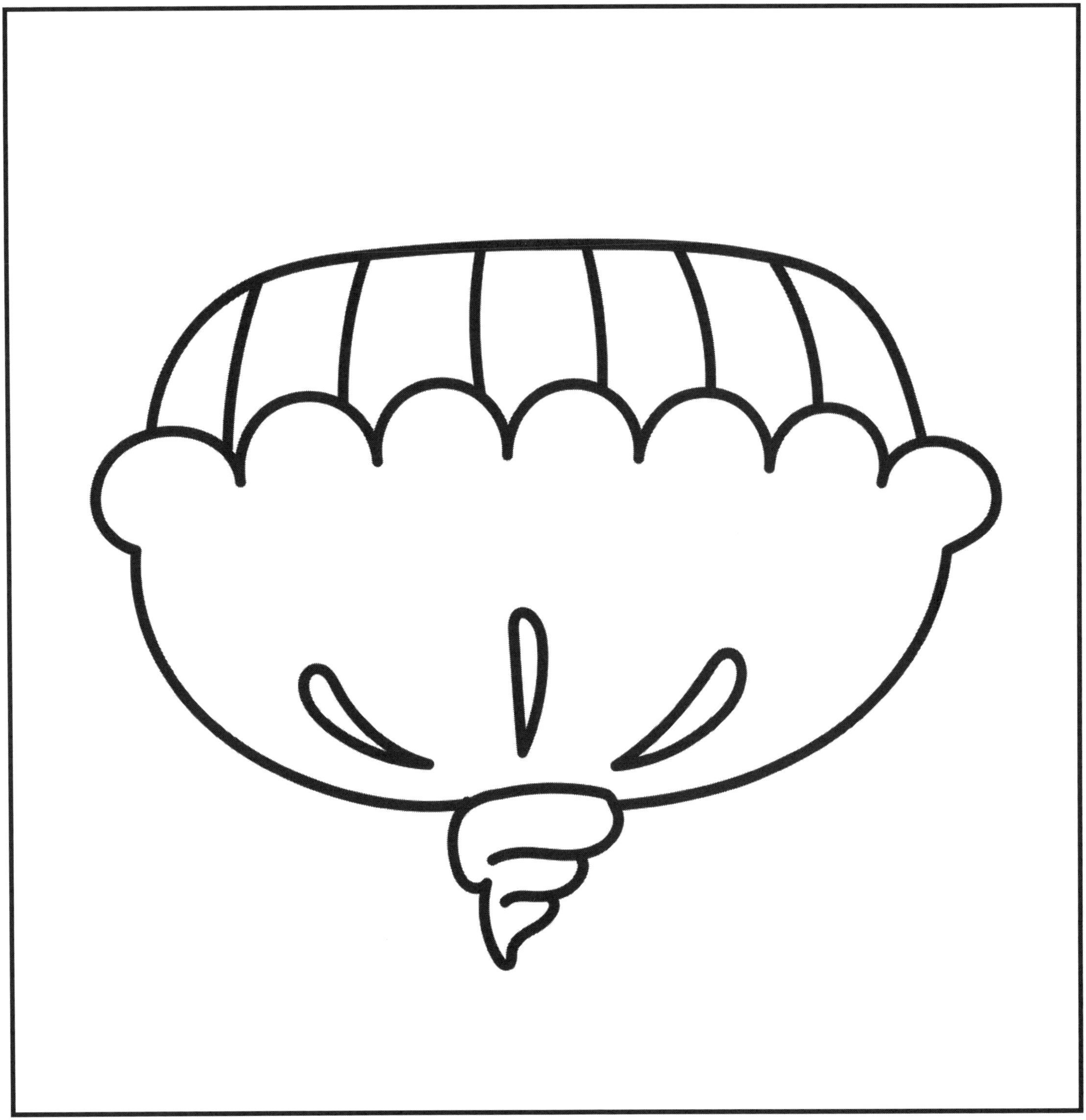

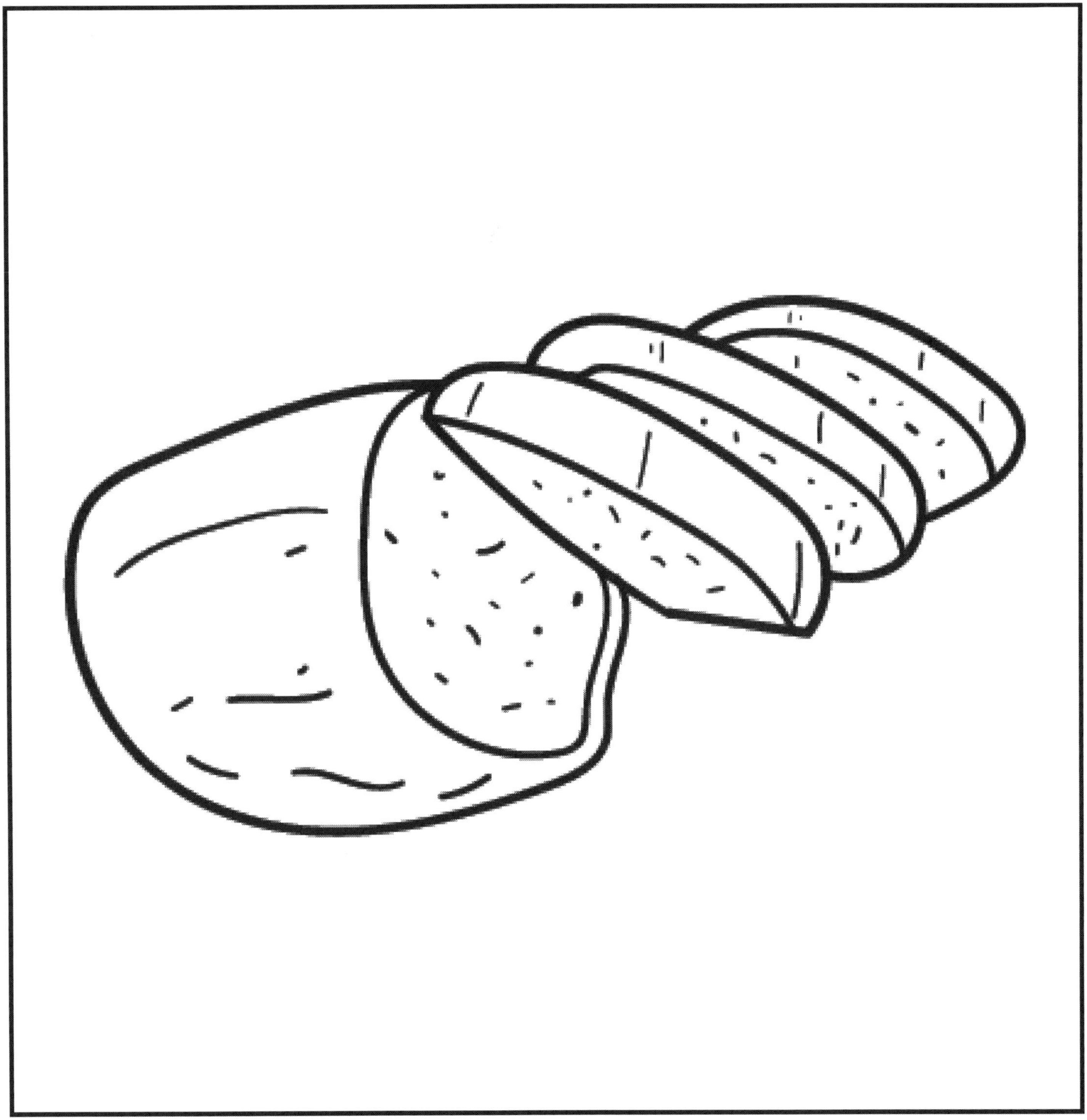

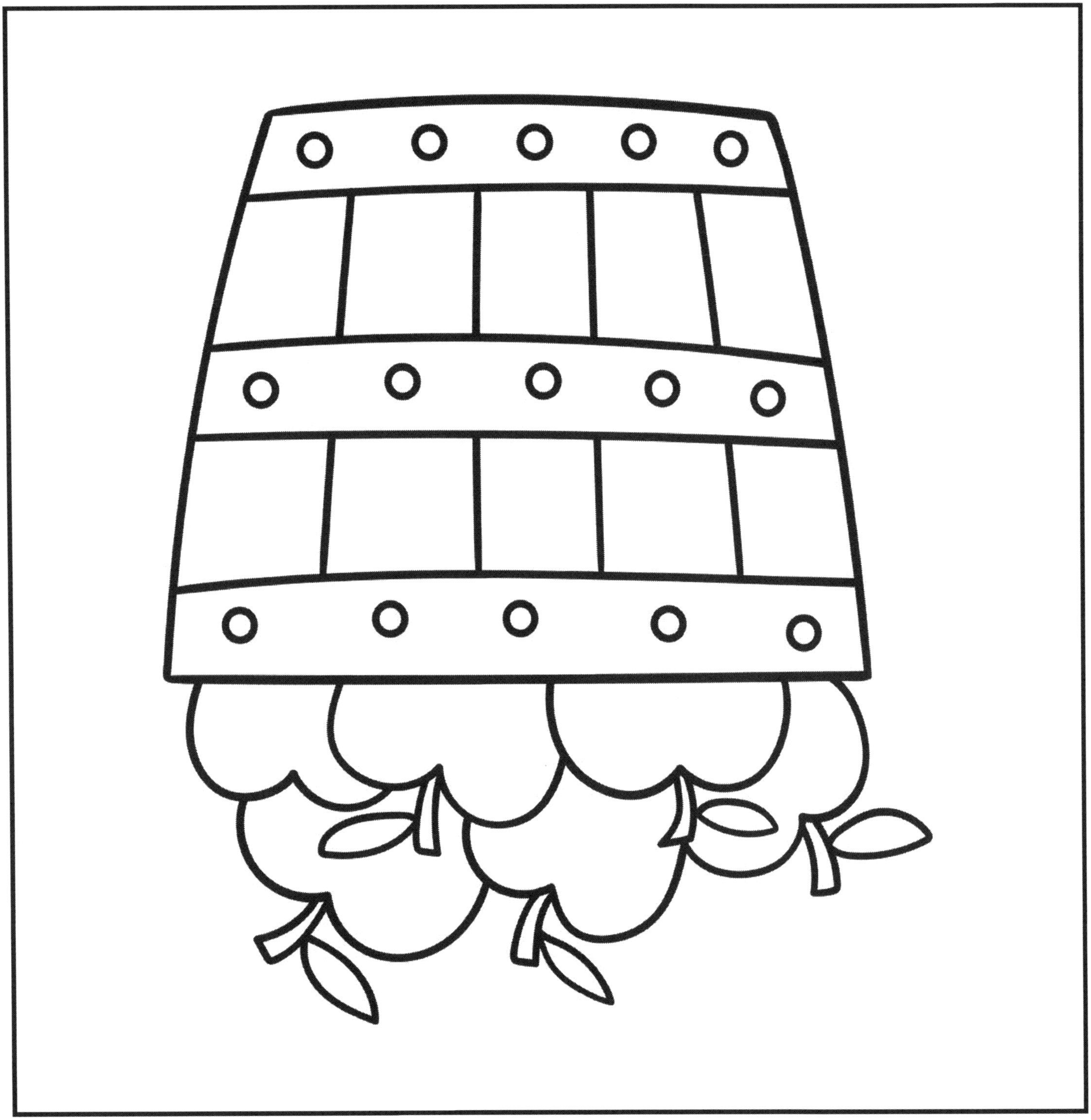

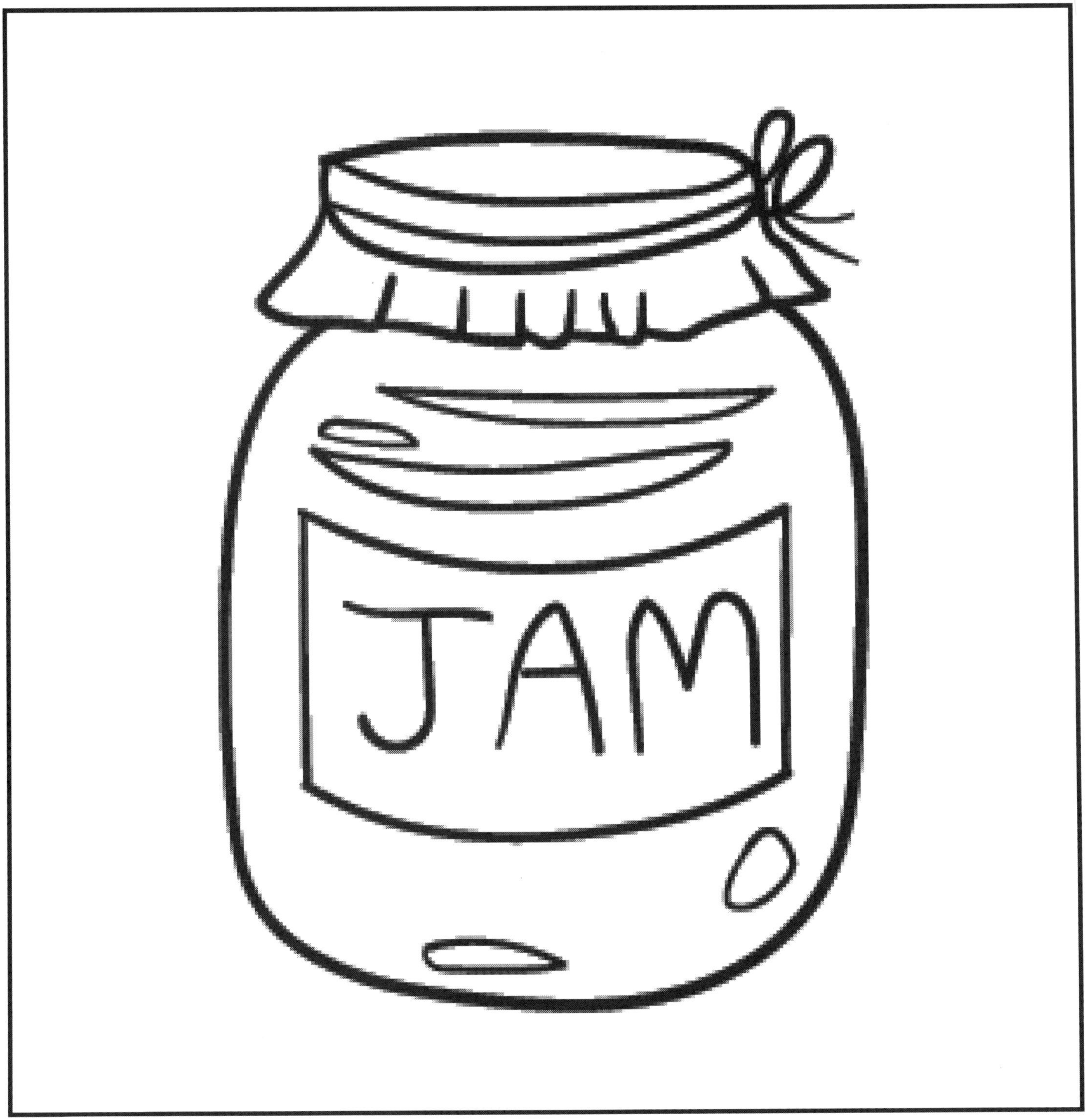
JAM

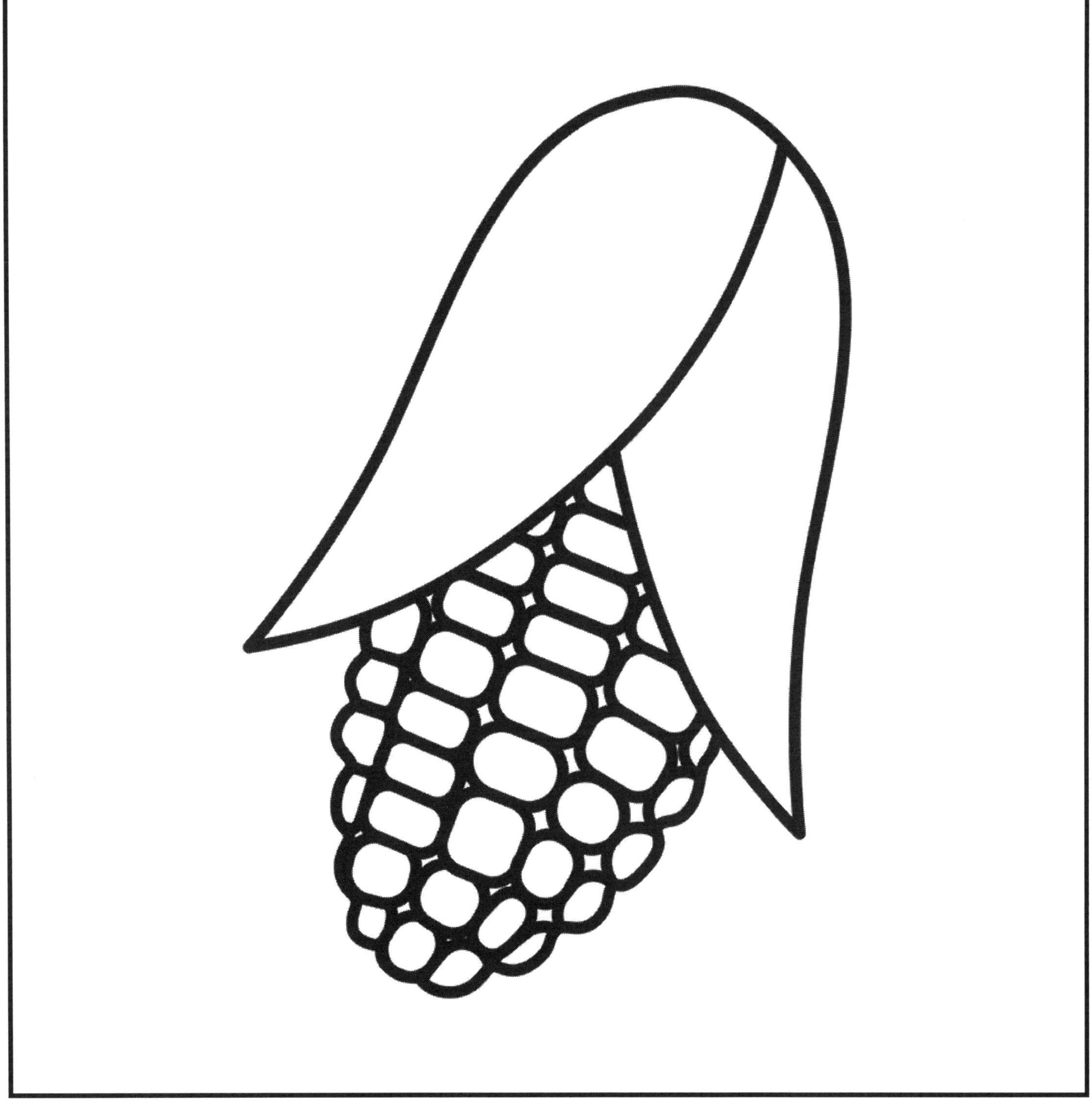

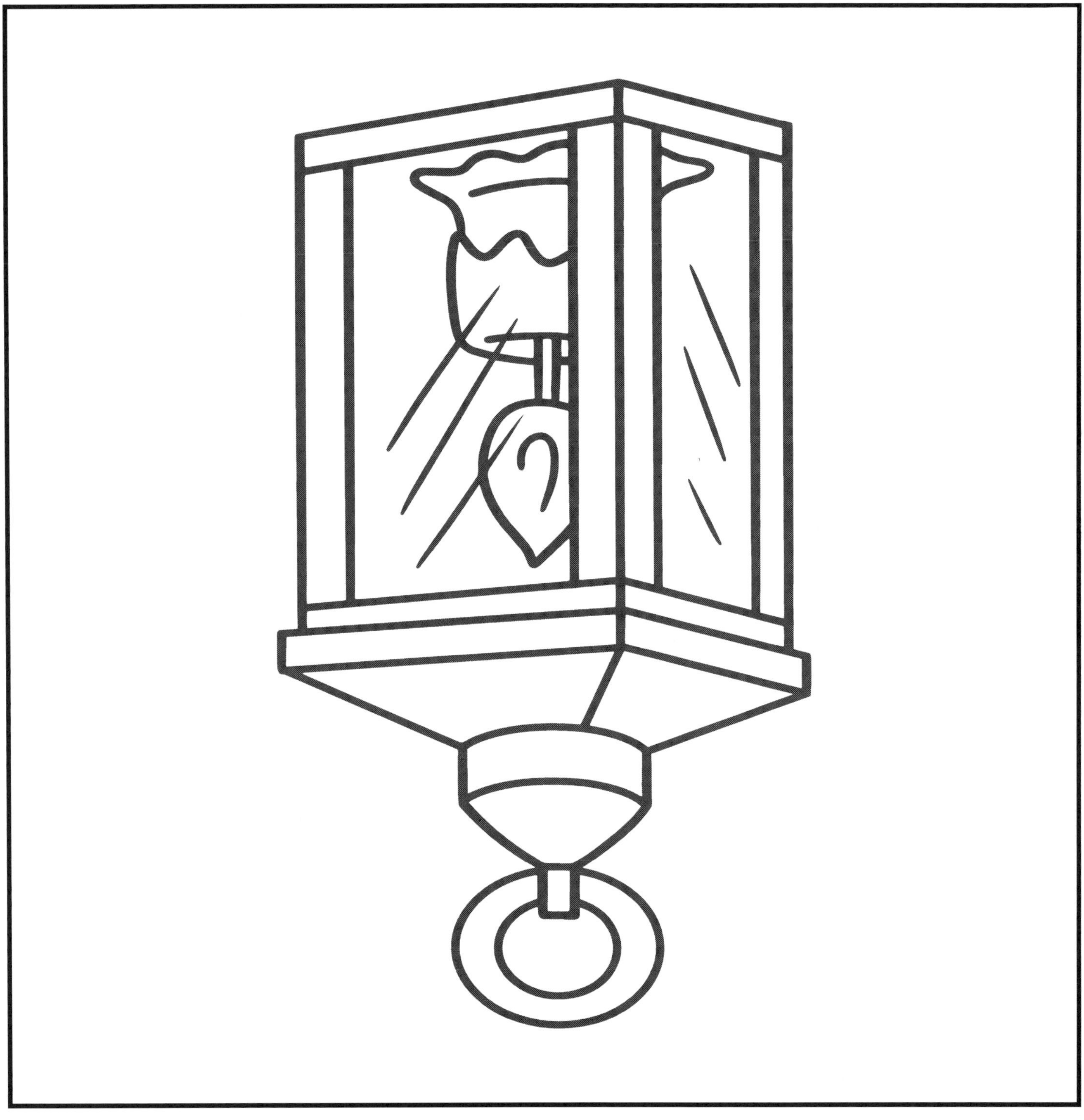

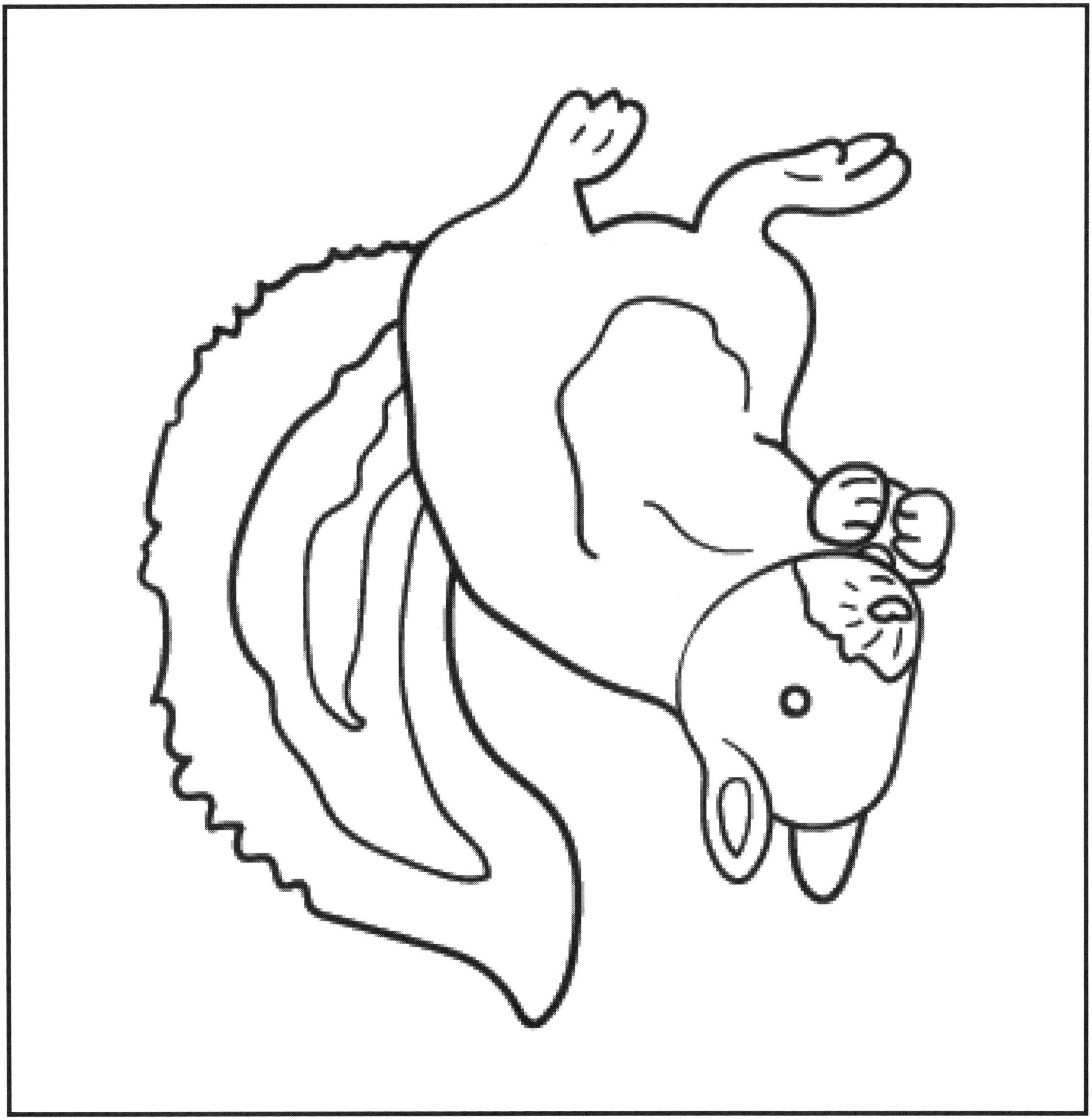

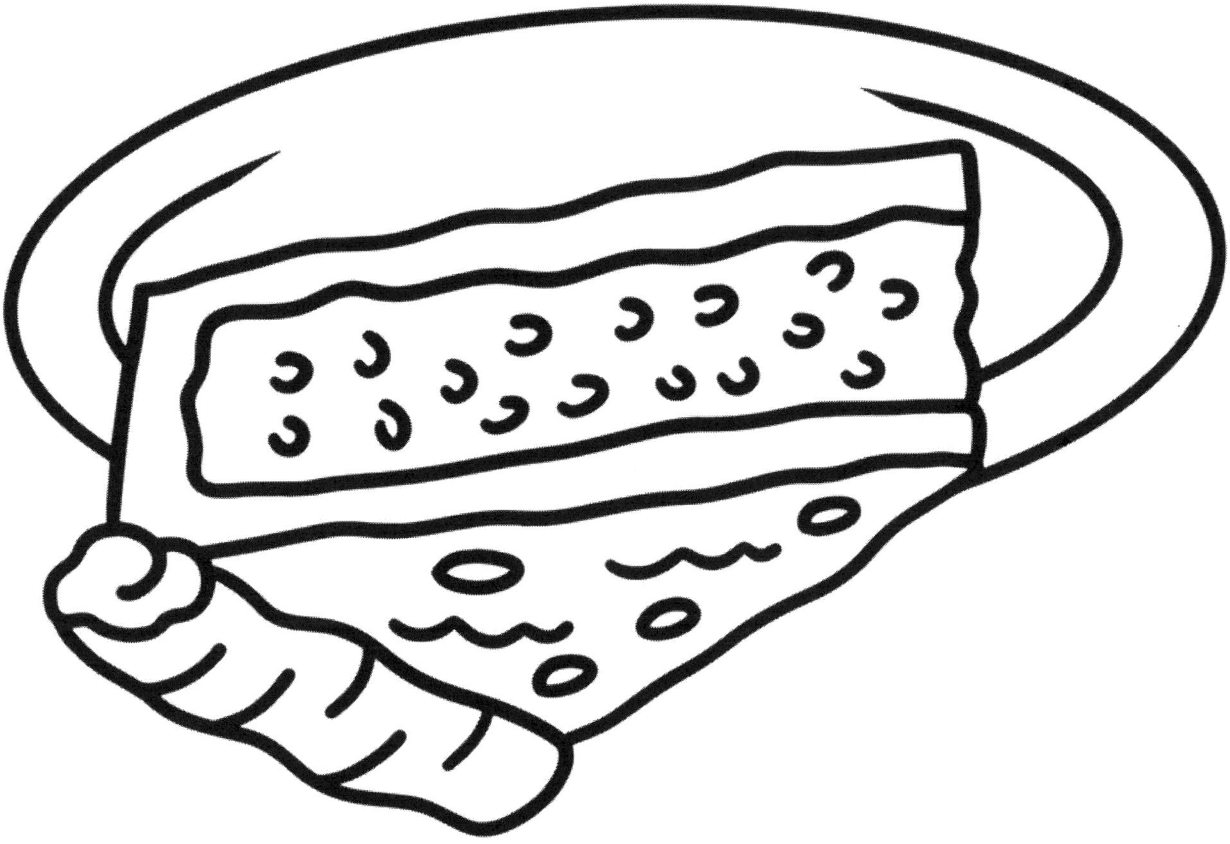

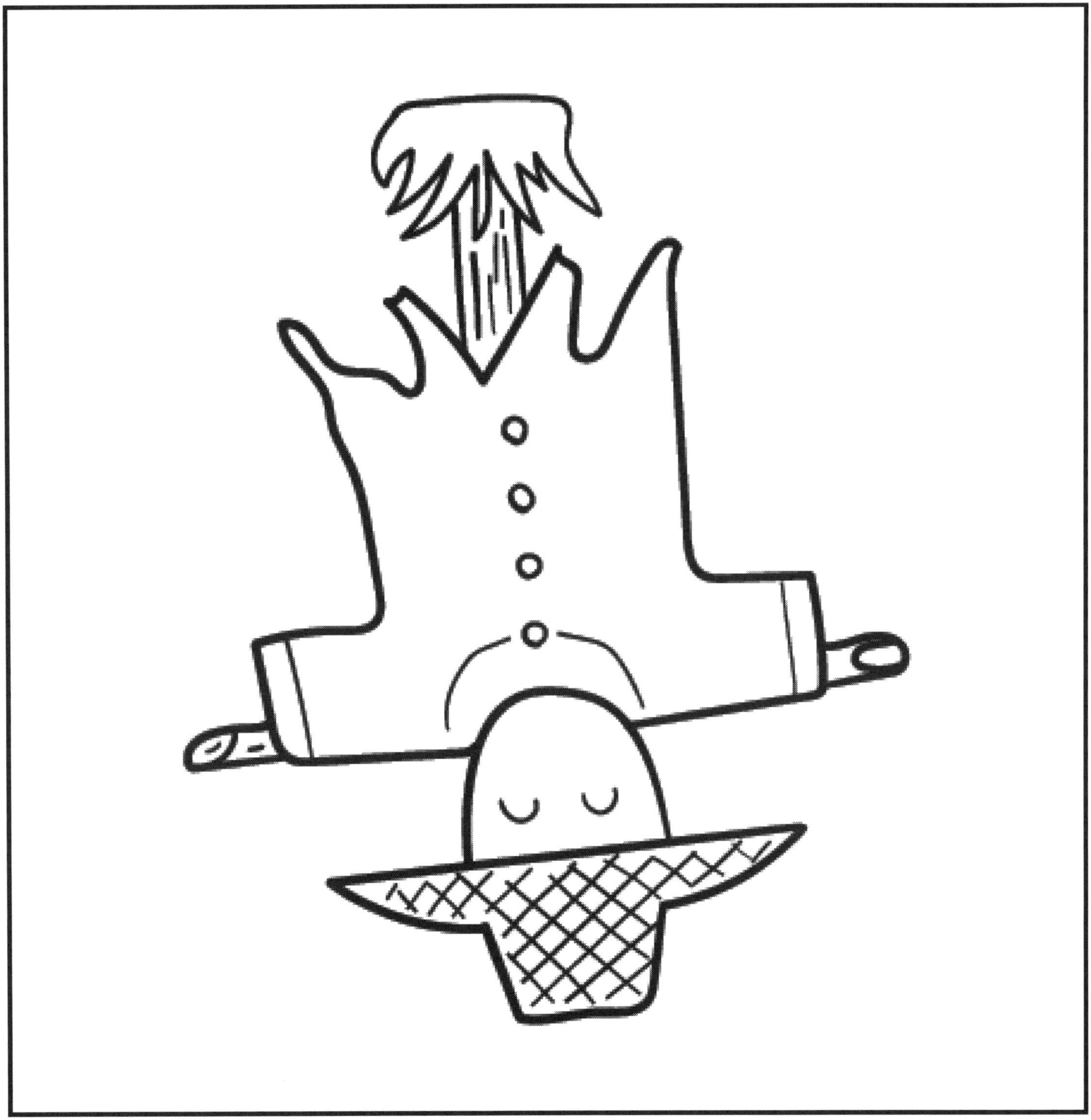

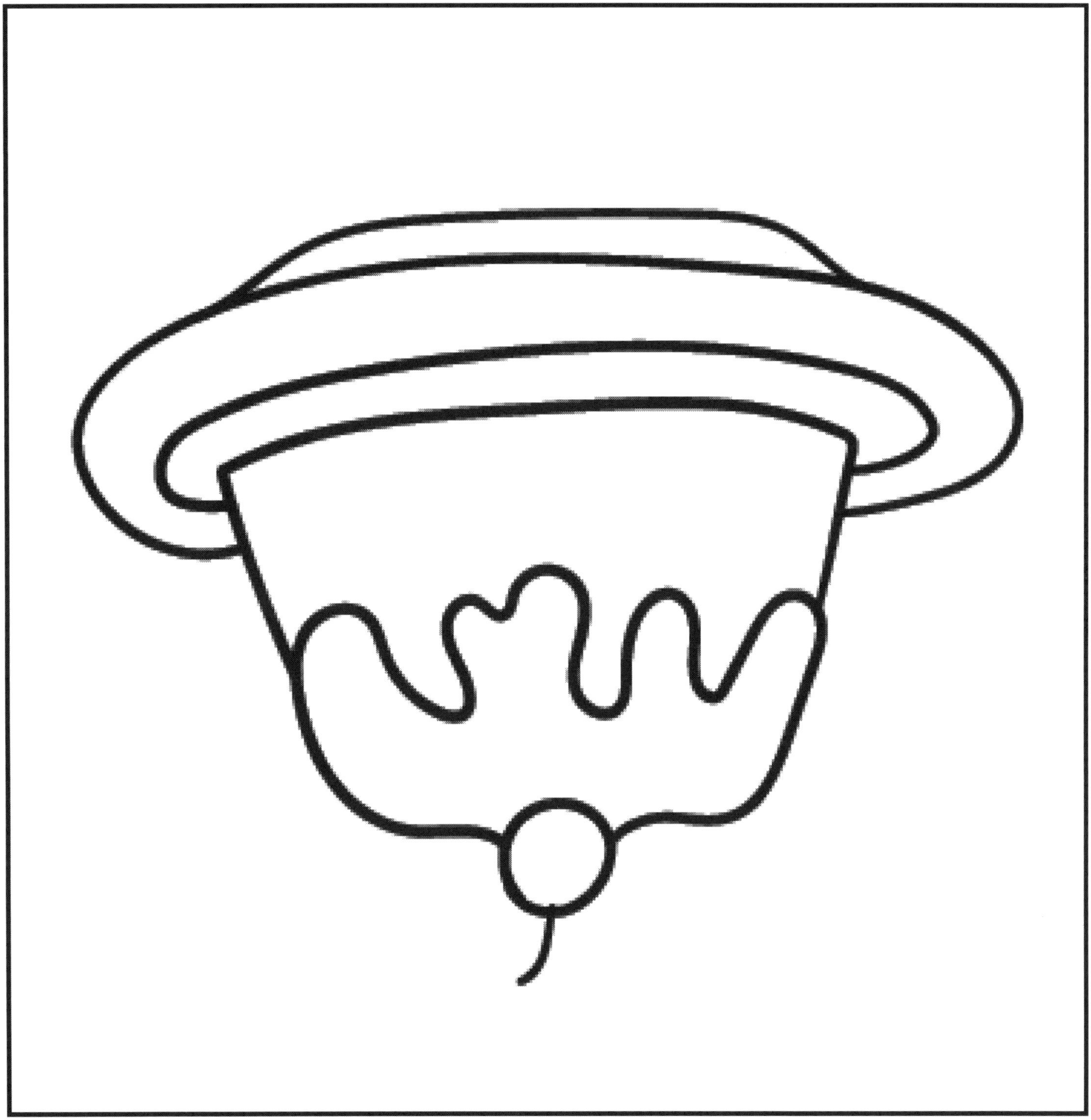

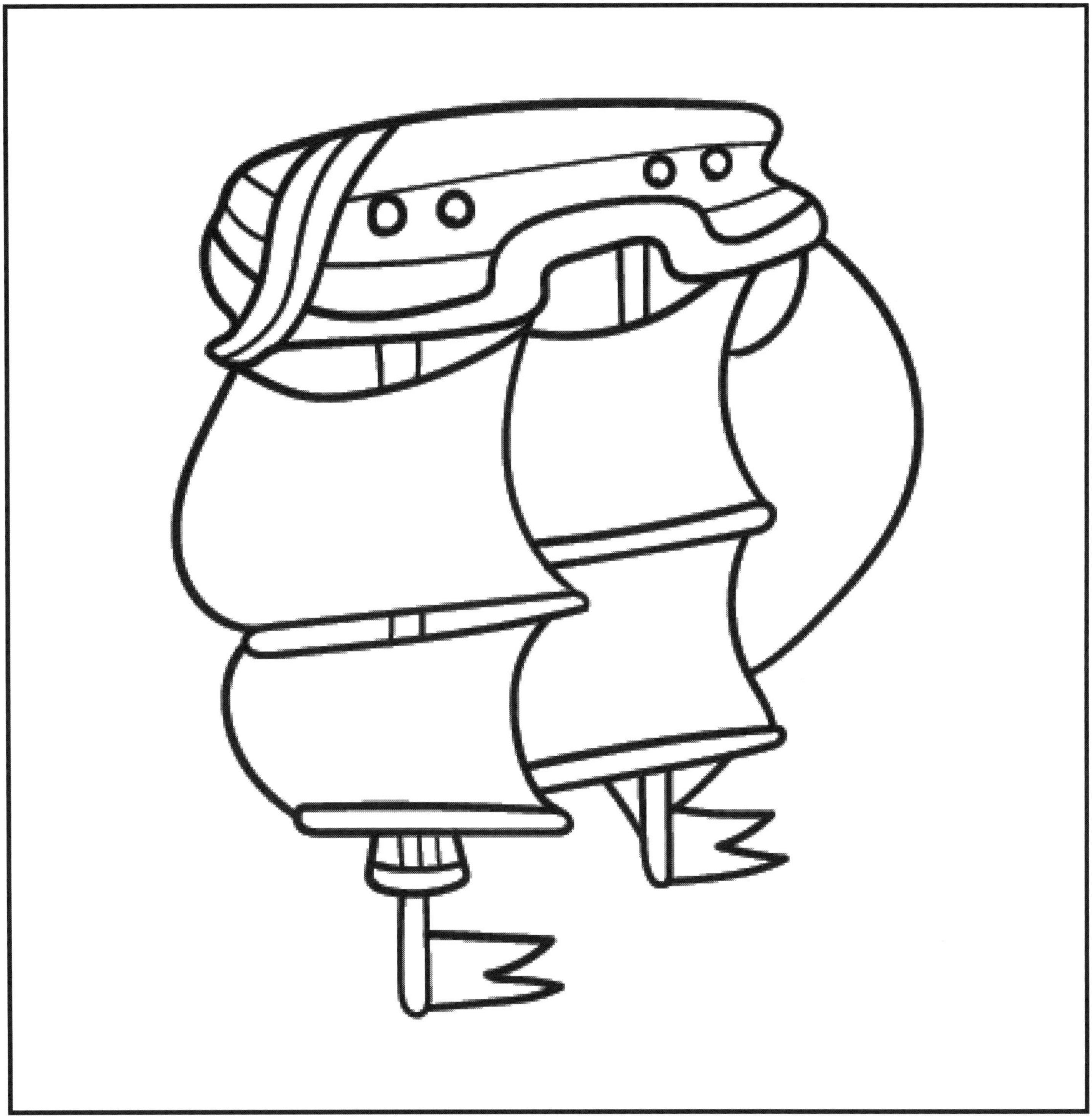

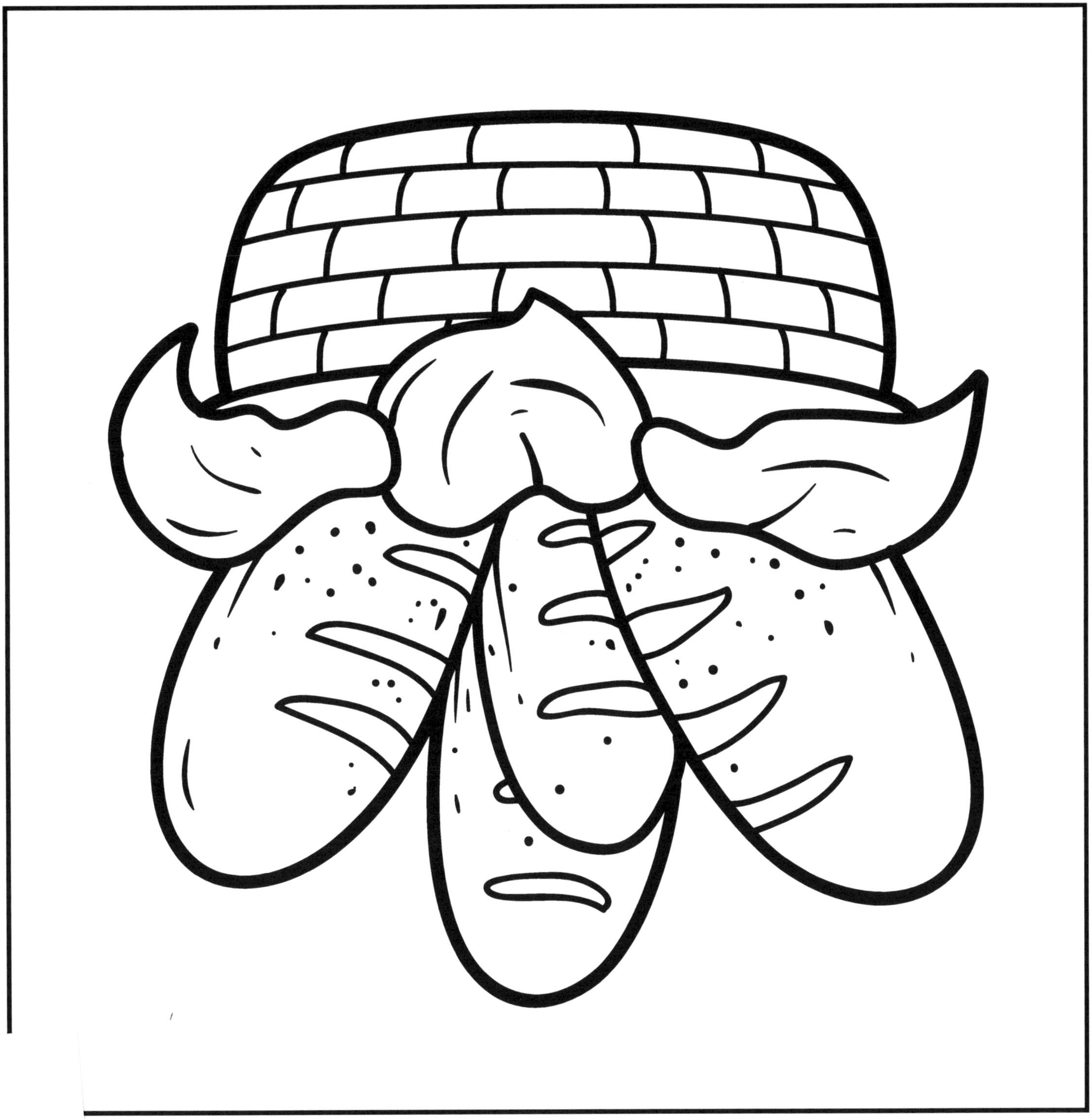

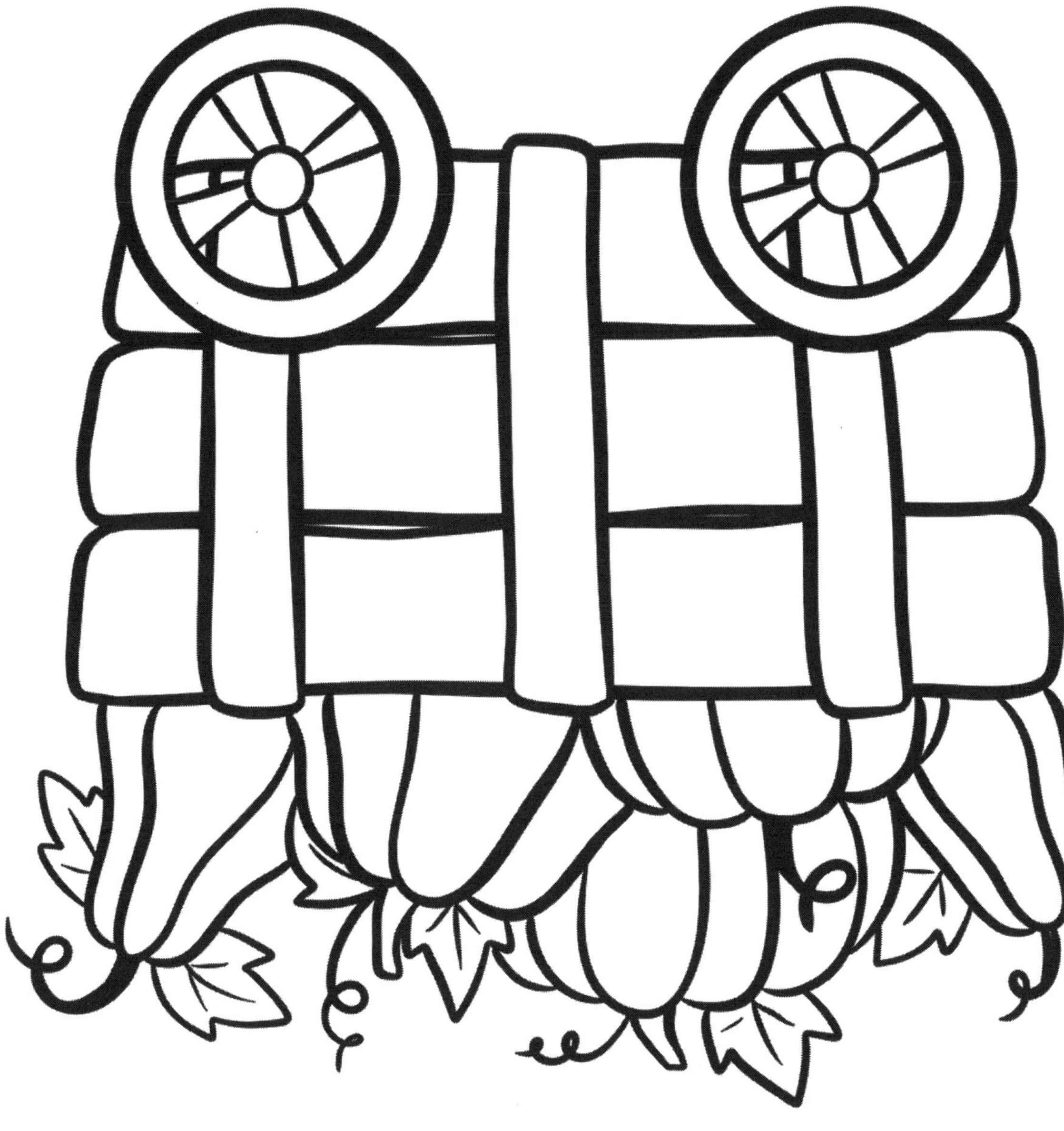

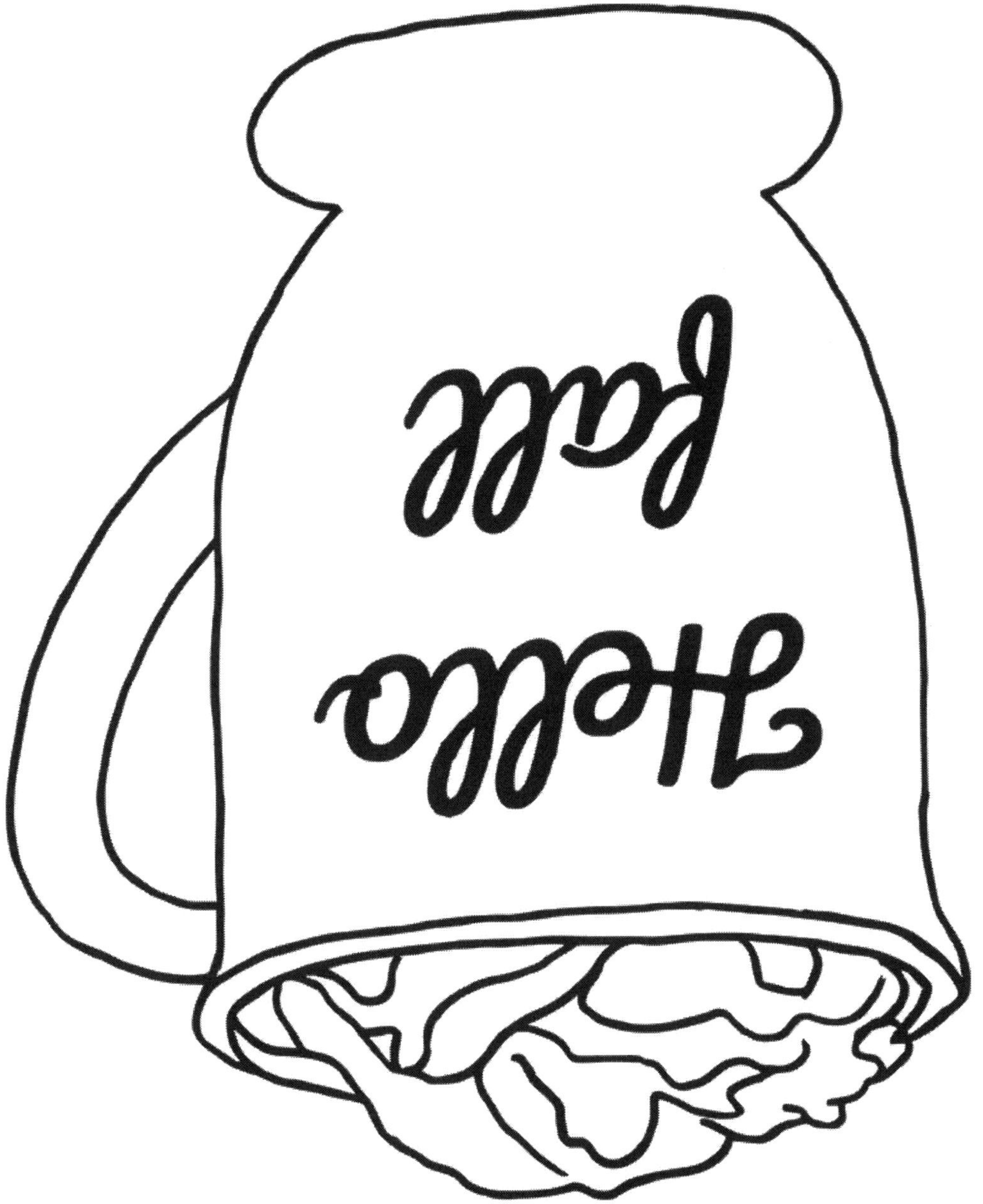
Hello
Fall

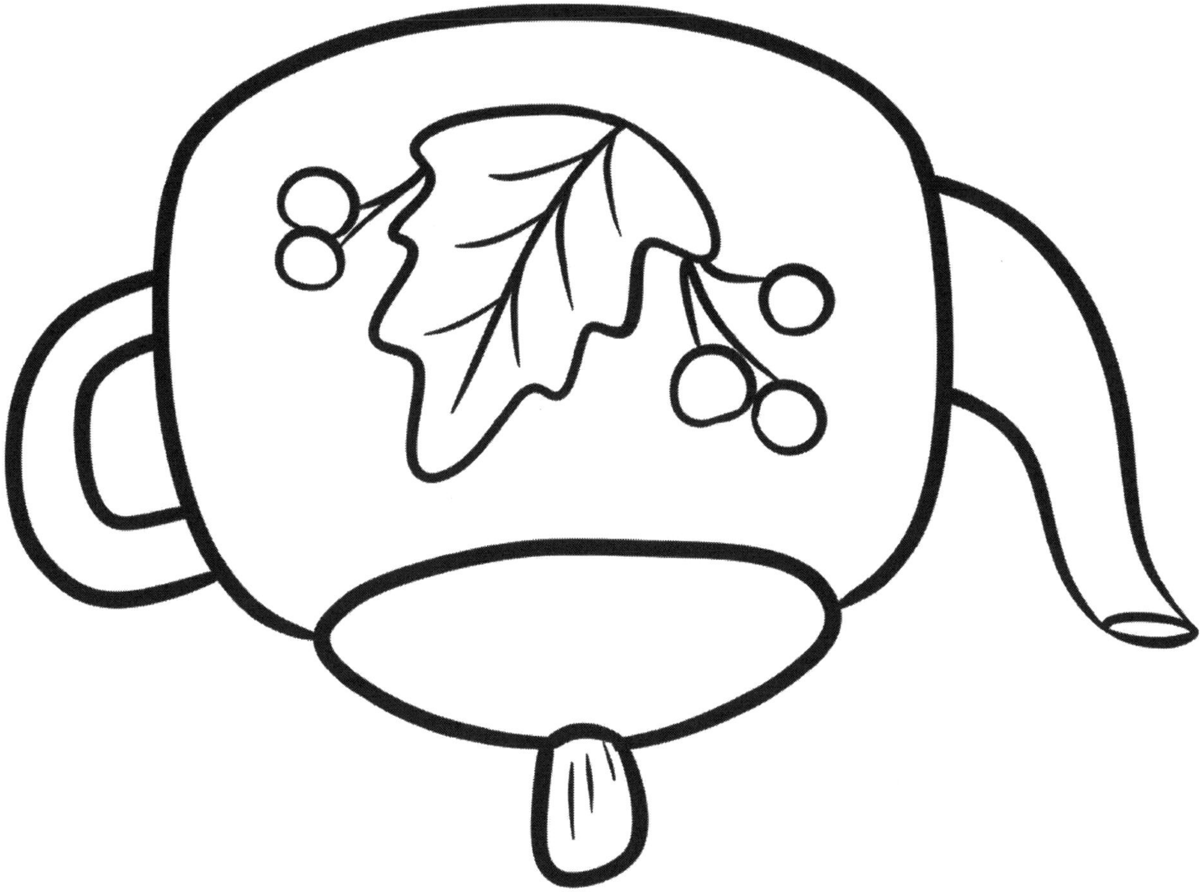

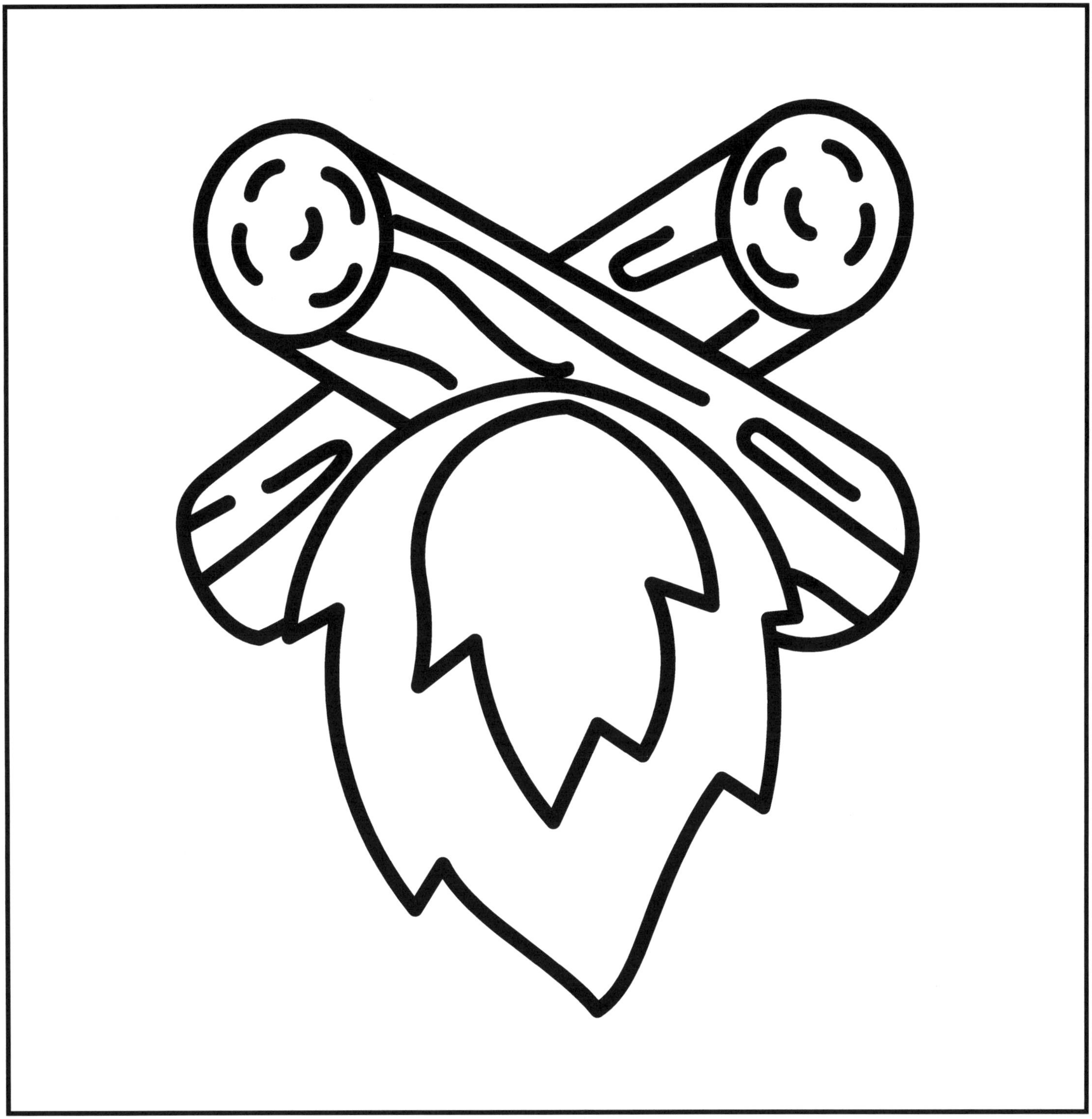

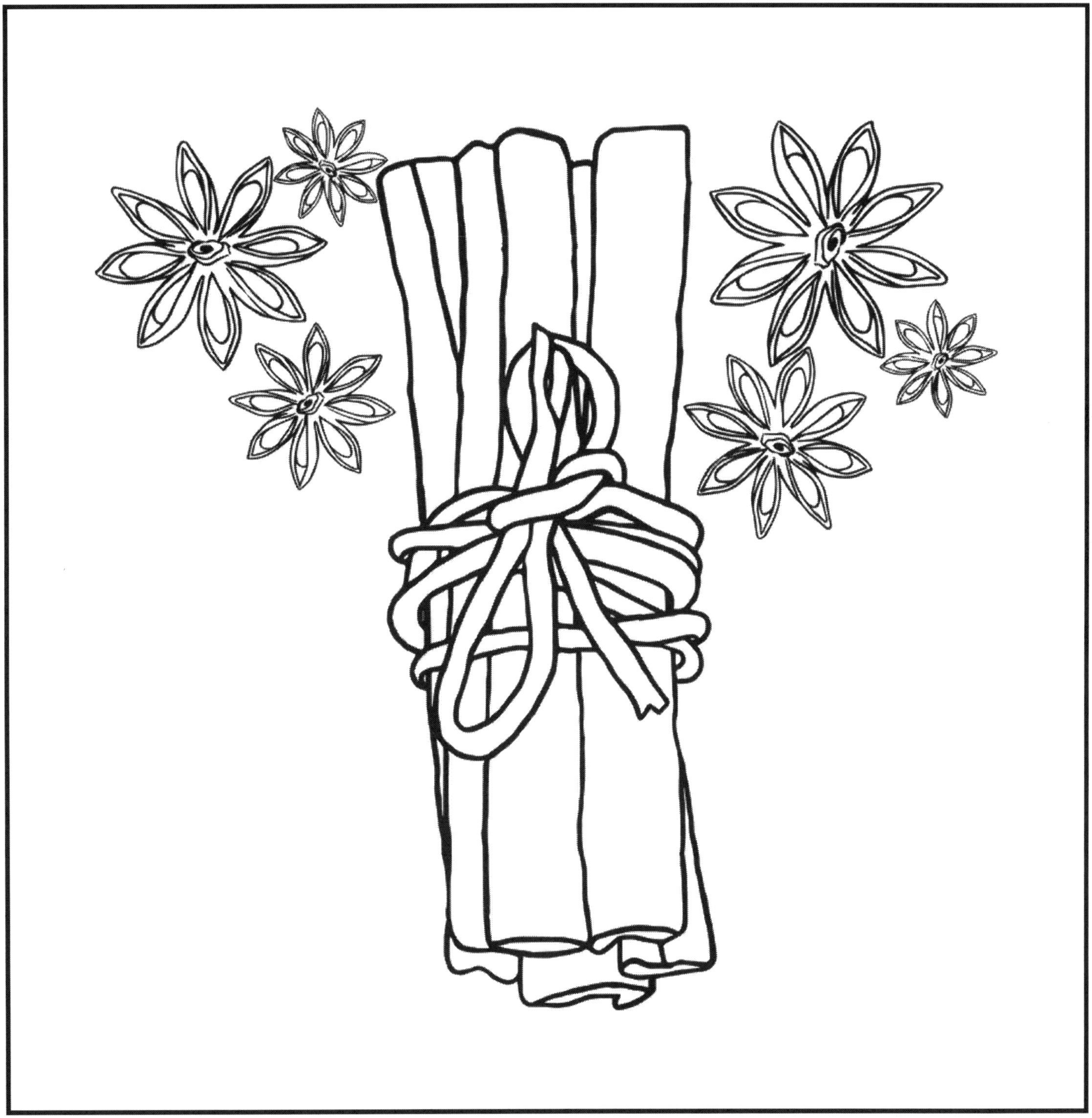

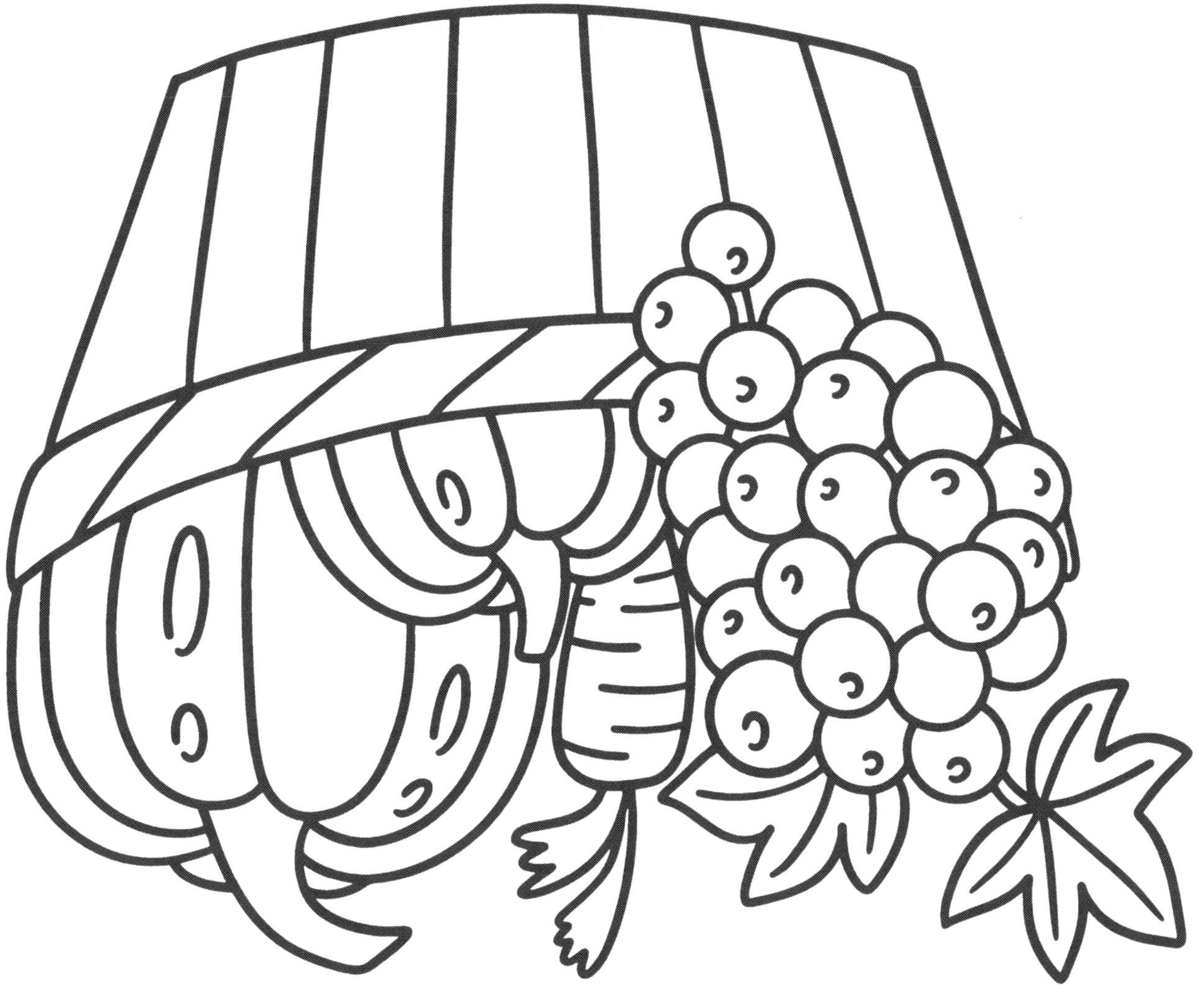

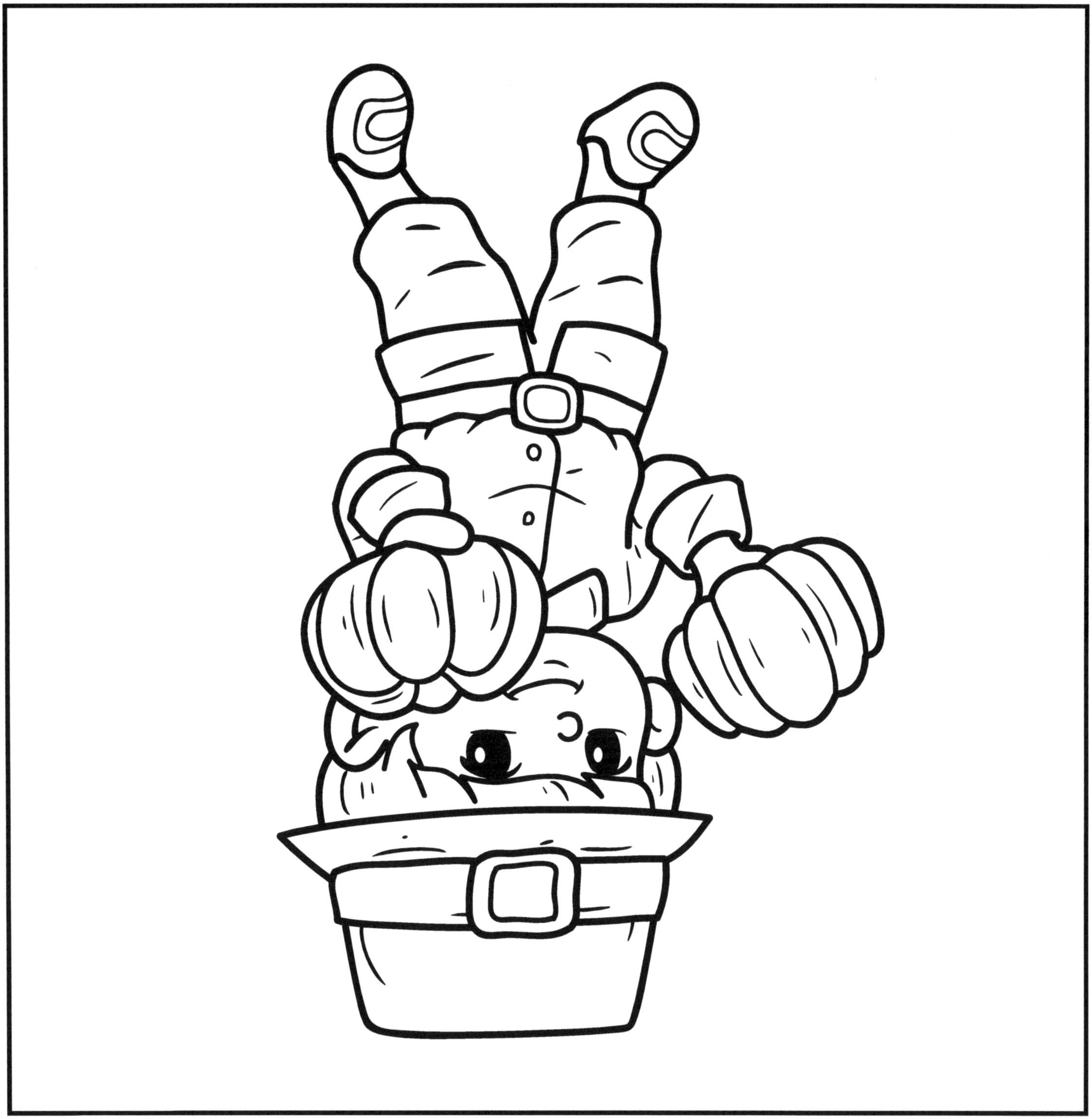

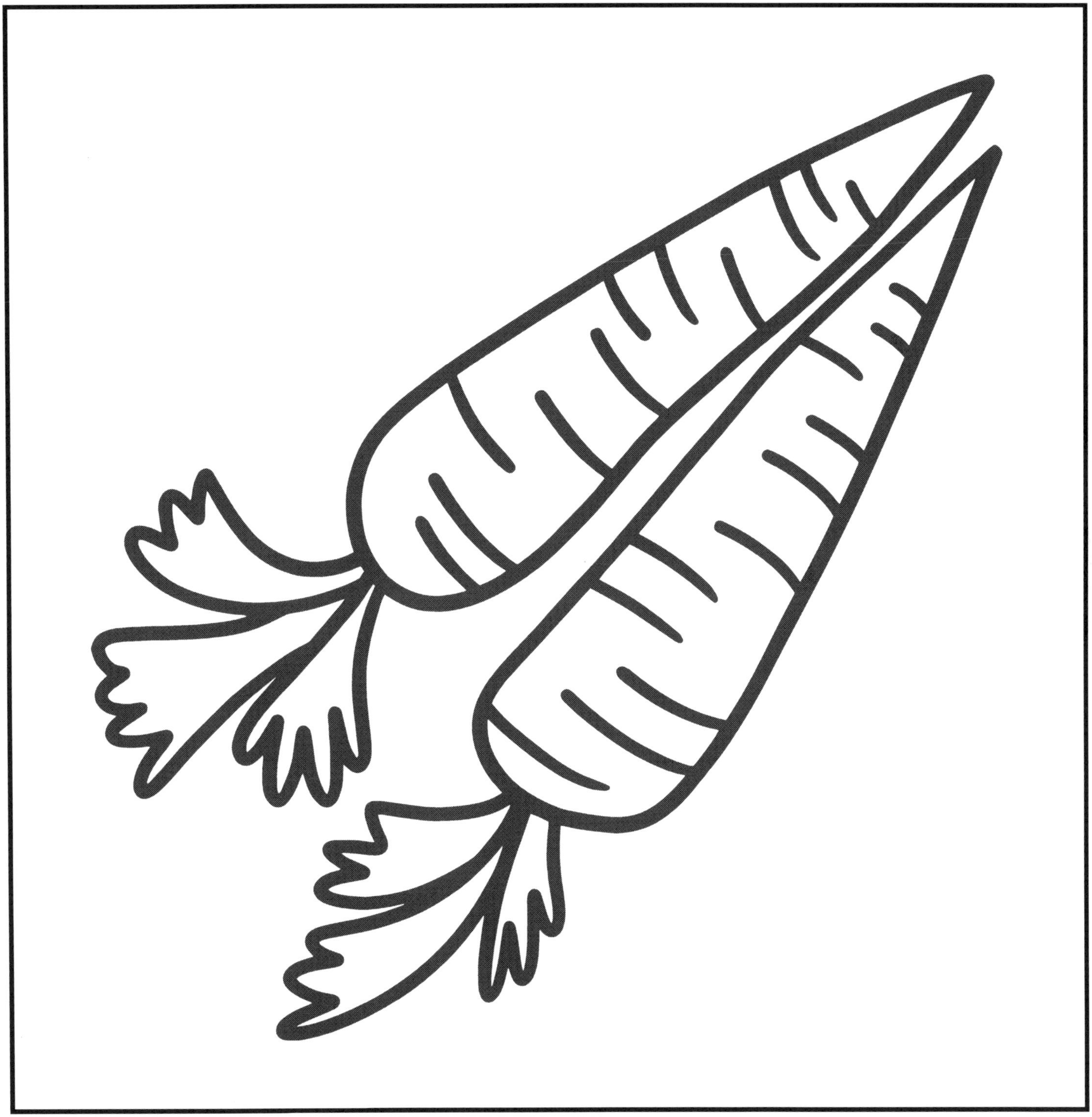

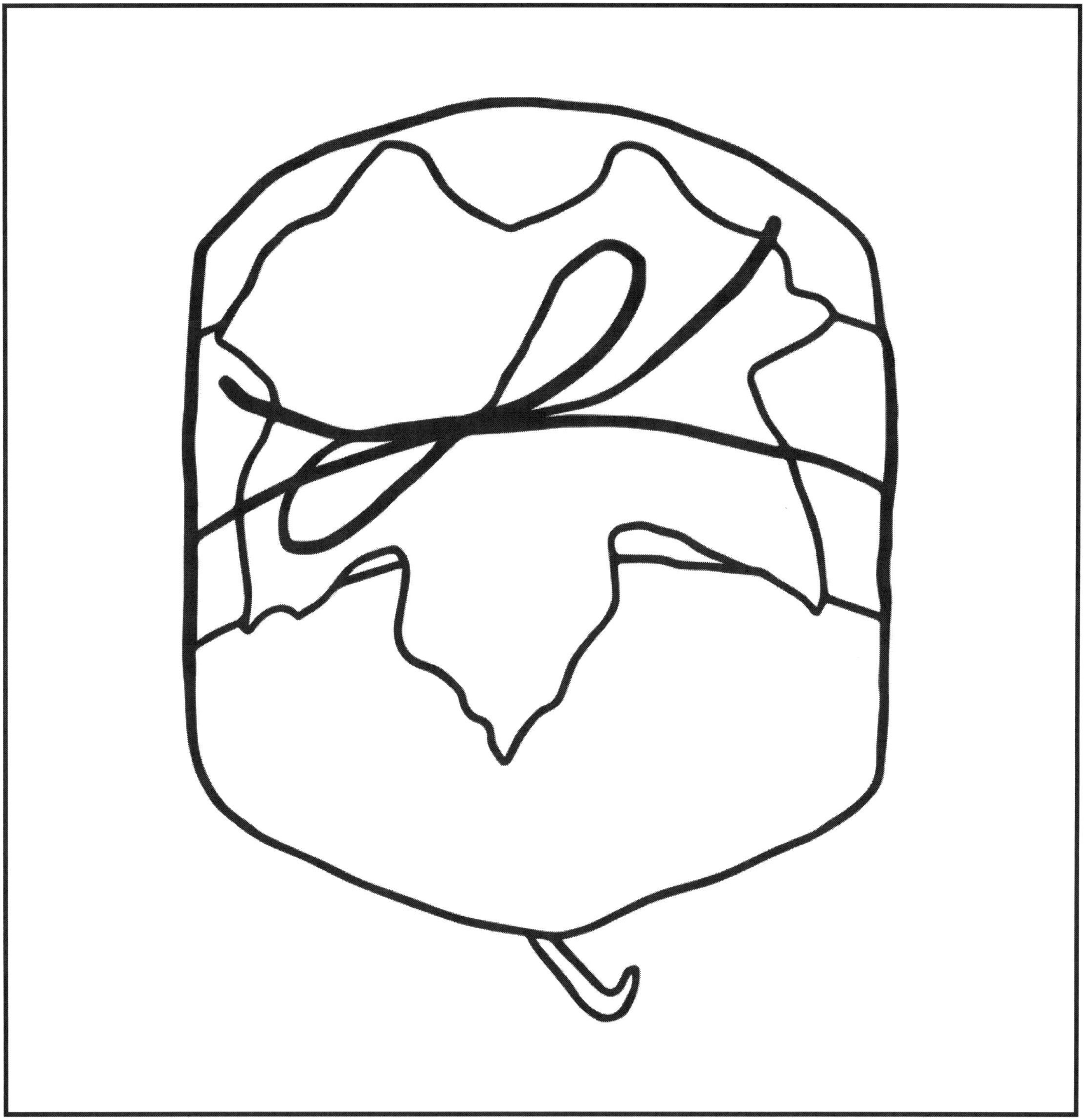

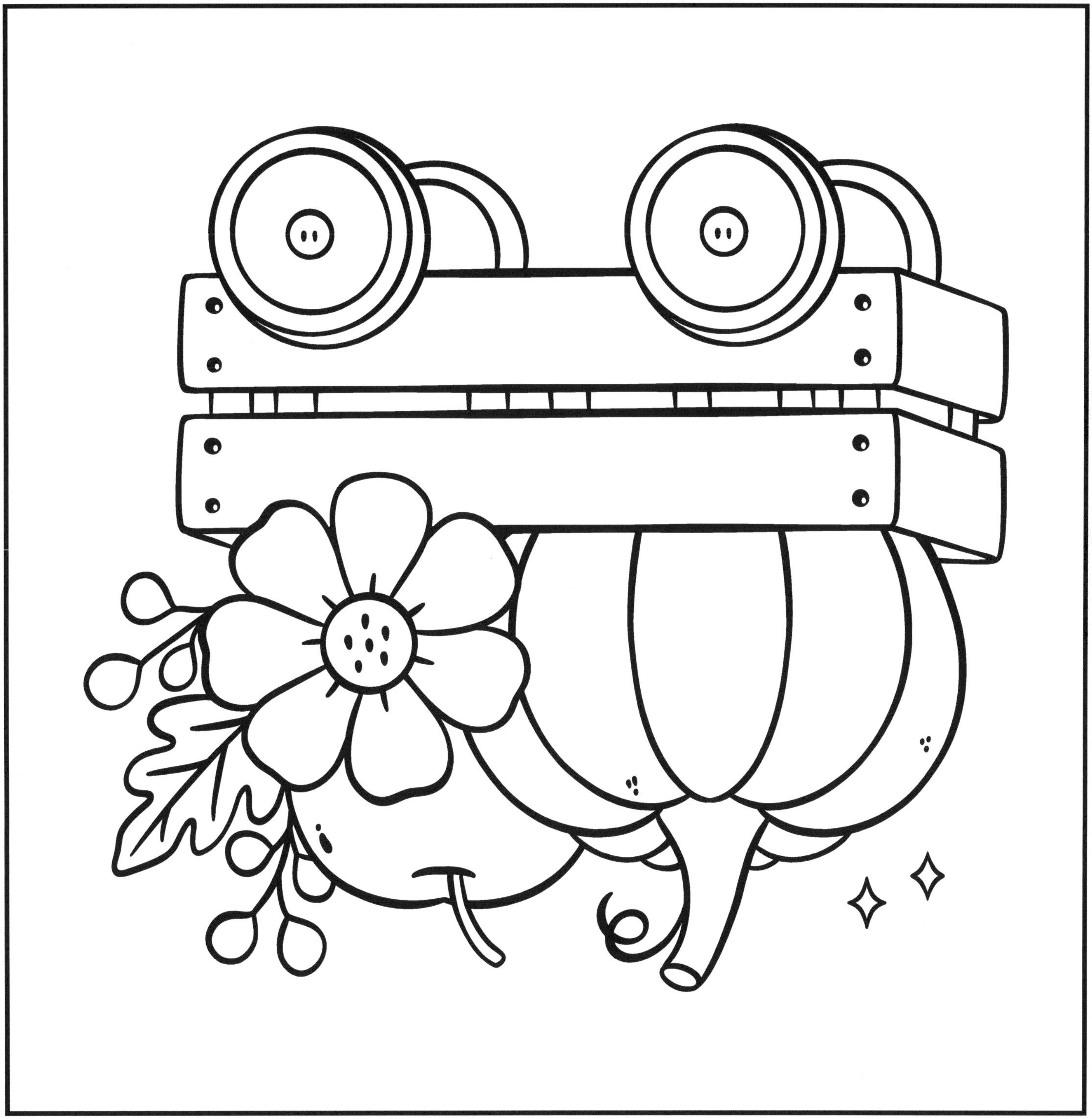

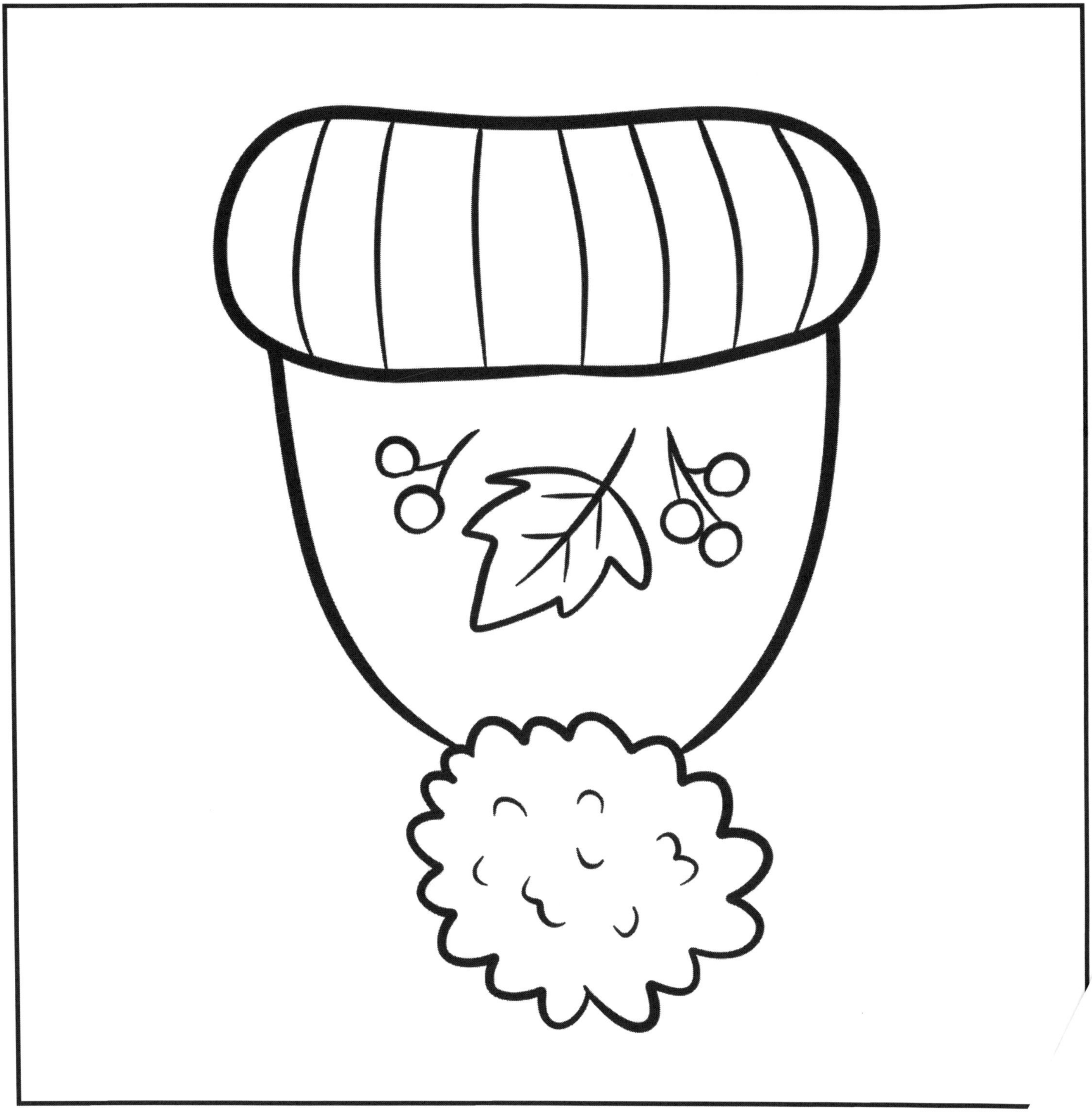

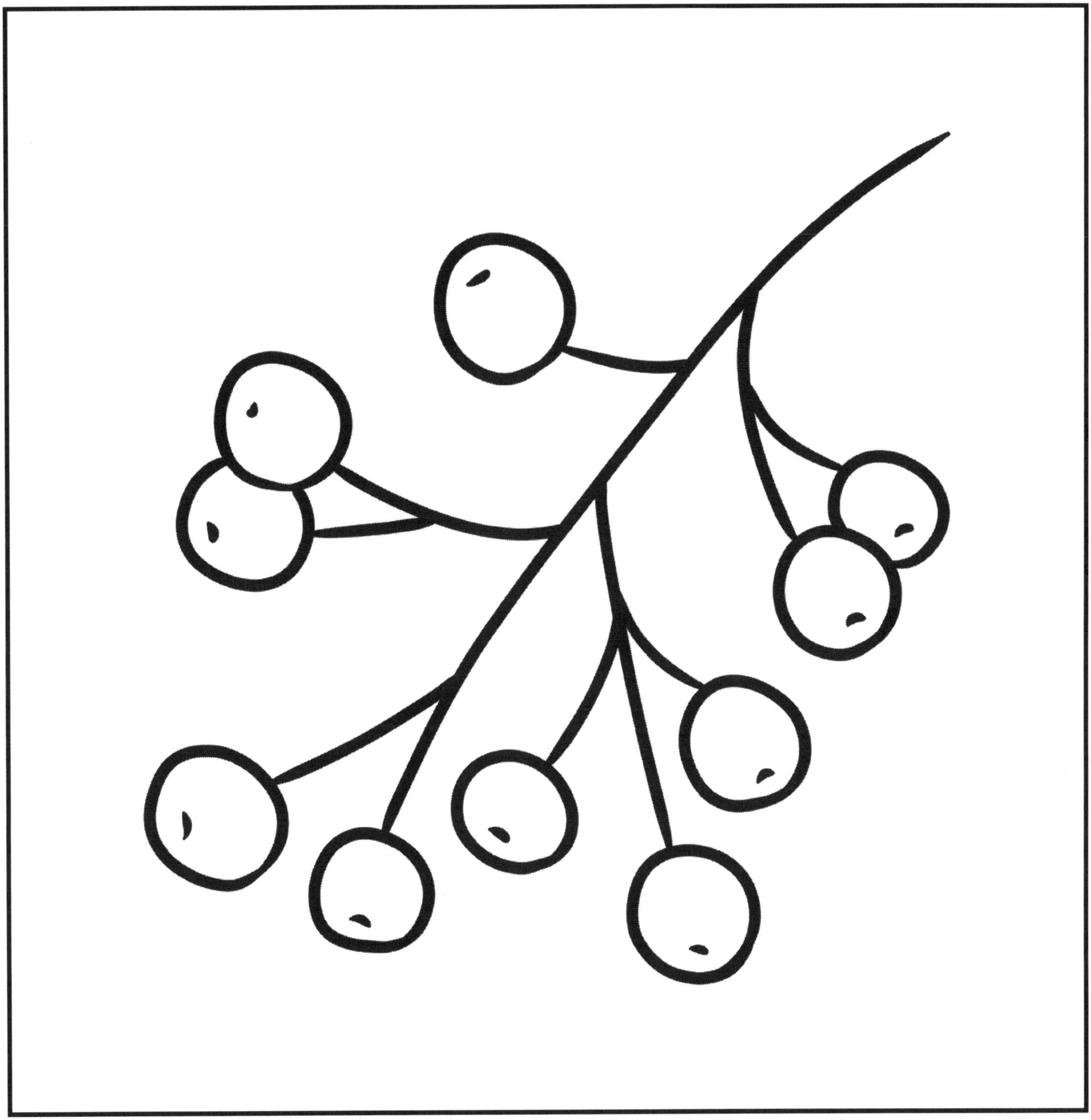

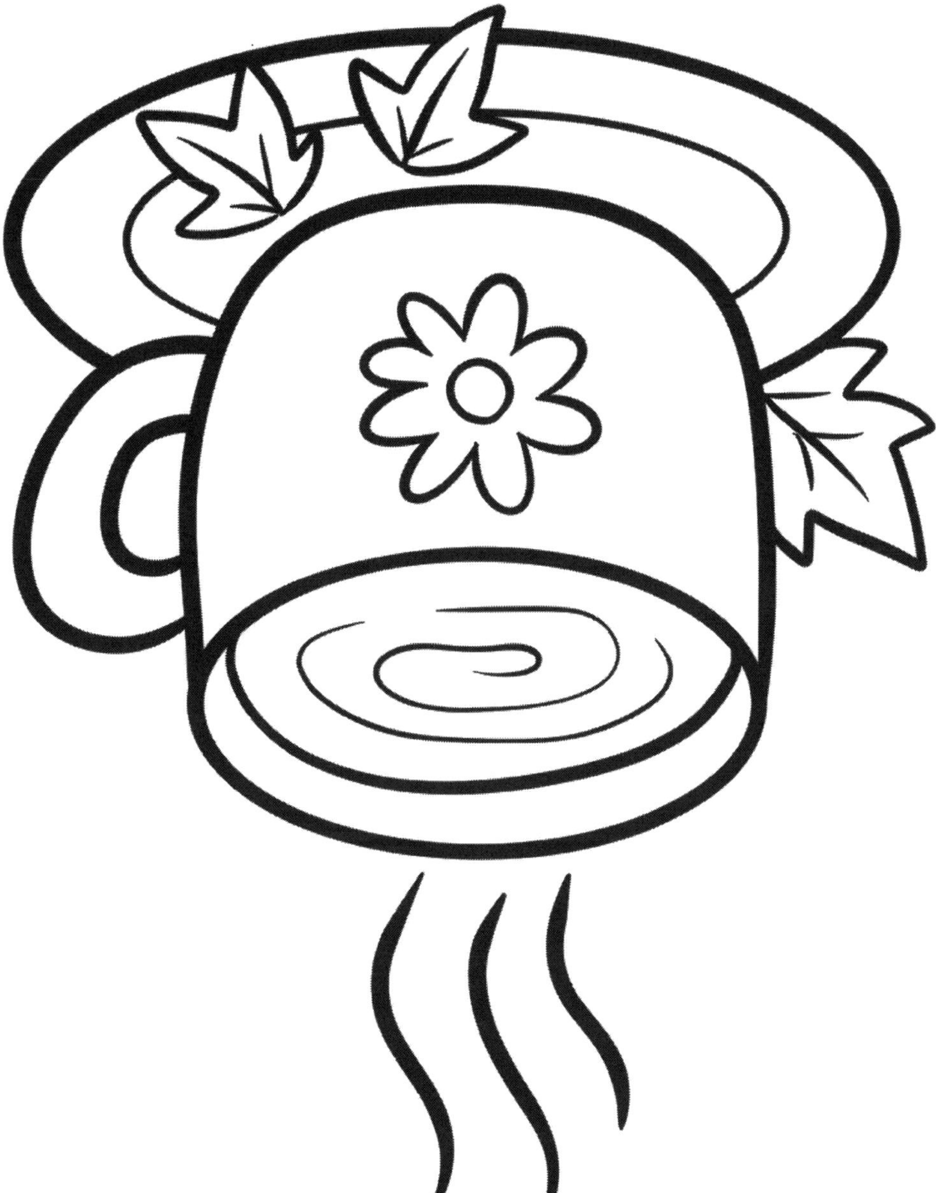

Thankful

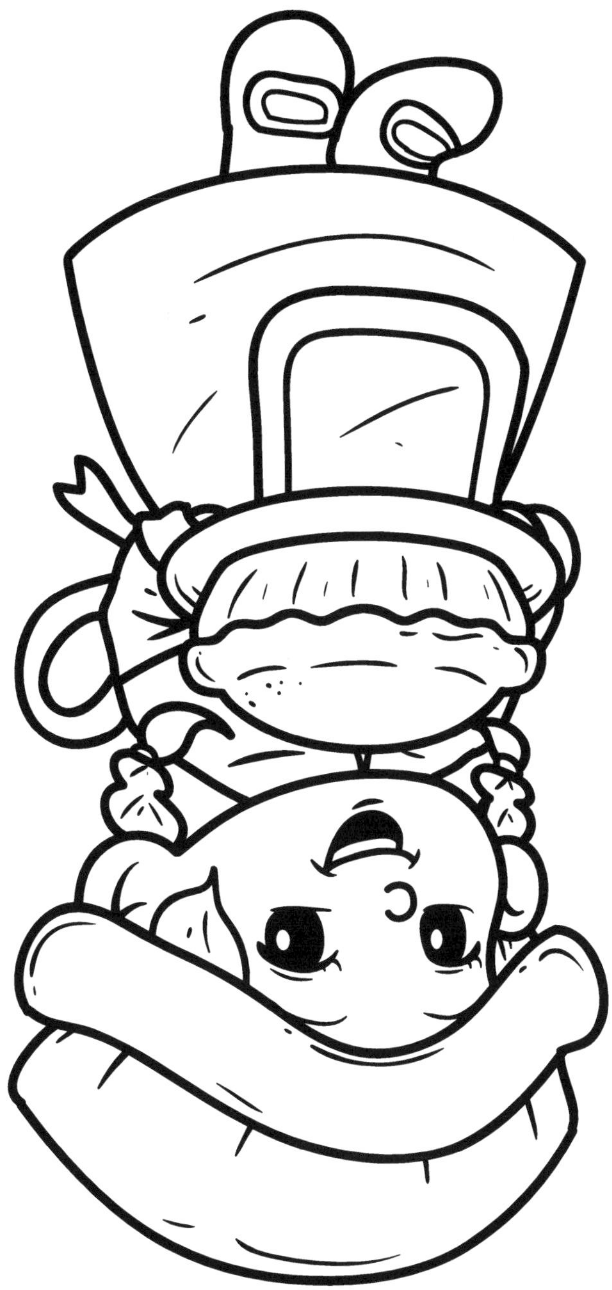

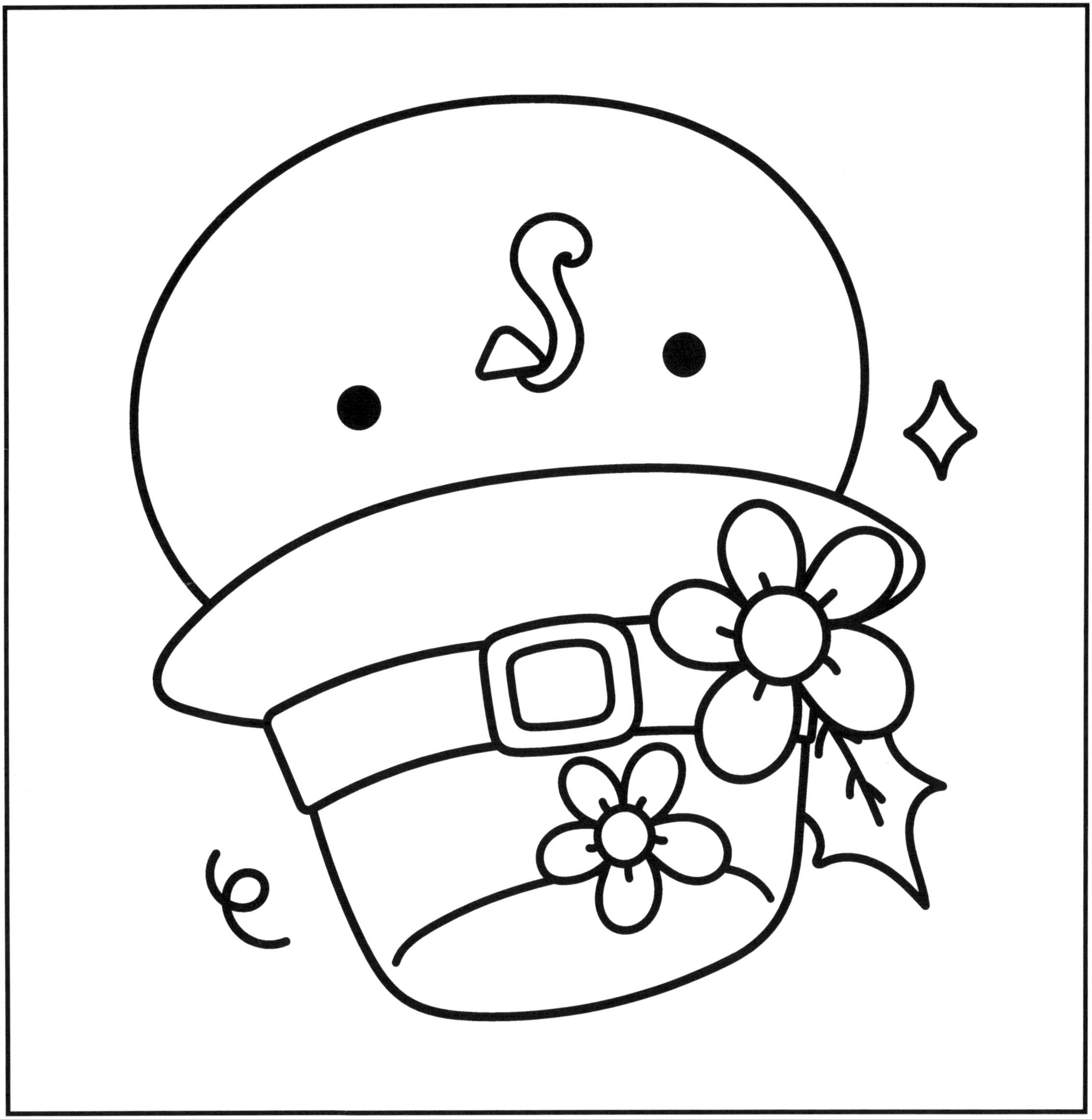

Made in United States
Orlando, FL
24 October 2024

53057955R00046